T0013911

'Why should Christians engage in [...] to be salt of the earth, light in th[...] neighbour means we are to get involved. Rooted in Scripture and prayer, this book brilliantly explains what that looks like in practice, how we can be compassionate without compromise in the fundamentals. It is part of a tradition that calls us to be "the King's good servant, but God's first" (Thomas More).'
Father Mark Vickers, author of *God in Number 10*

'This book offers a refreshingly honest, brave, insightful and reasoned account of Christian engagement in politics. It avoids being either naive or cynical. It draws on outstanding scholarship and provides practical wisdom. It not only argues that the gospel relates to all of life, including politics, but considers the challenges and opportunities of taking such a claim seriously. Politics is indeed a mucky business, and one in which we must play our part if we are serious about loving God and loving our neighbours as ourselves.'
Paul Woolley, CEO, the London Institute for Contemporary Christianity

'A fantastic read, *A Mucky Business* shows that social injustice should be on the heart of every Christian. Politics and the gospel are entwined in giving the world the good news of Jesus Christ. The different conversations in this book all speak the same language. Tim blends the text in such a way that the reader wants more.'
Pastor Mick Fleming, leader of Church on the Street Ministries in Burnley, and author of *Blown Away: From drug dealer to life bringer*

'Tim Farron is a hero of mine, and I'm so glad he's written a book that will help Christians pursue faithfulness in all of life, including politics! I trust this book will be a great encouragement to all who have grown weary of our politics, and I believe it will empower Christians to make a difference for good.'
Michael Wear, author of *Reclaiming Hope: Lessons Learned in the Obama White House About the Future of Faith in America*

'What an important book! Here is a Bible-based, down-to-earth guide to why and how Christians should be involved in politics and the public square. It is written with warmth, wisdom, humour, compassion and a deep practical knowledge of the subject from many years of service at the heart of UK politics. I hope it will help inspire and equip a new generation of servant-hearted Christians to get involved in politics, from community level right up to government level.'
Philippa Taylor, director of the CARE Leadership Programme

'Jesus didn't run away from the muck. He waded straight into it, but in the knowledge that he was doing what his Father was calling him to. If you've been trying to keep your feet clean by avoiding the muck of the public square (both online and offline), this is the book for you. It will help you get stuck in, but also understand why and for whom you're suddenly knee-deep.'
Andy Flannagan, executive director of Christians in Politics

'With charm, honesty and conviction, Tim Farron explores the tensions that are conventionally thought to lie between Christian faith and the practice of politics, and demonstrates that there need be no tension at all.'
Tom Holland, historian and author of *Dominion: The making of the Western mind*

'There are few people better-placed than Tim Farron to advise people of faith on the opportunities and perils of political engagement. Tim and his co-authors are realistic about what politics is, but also hopeful that there is good work to be done by Christians in the public square. This book doesn't offer political theory, but a biblically informed political practice. Any Christian who senses a call to public life should read it.
Paul Bickley, acting head of research at Theos

'This book has its head in a theological vision for cultural engagement and its feet firmly planted in the mucky business of political

life. Like Tim Farron himself, it is ebullient, principled, astute and hopeful in all the right ways.'
Glen Scrivener, director and evangelist at Speak Life, and author of *The Air We Breathe*

'Tim Farron's book is a timely antidote, both to widespread apathy about involvement in social issues and to frustration with the deceptions and intrigues of politicians. Here is an active politician who is honest about his Christian beliefs as well as his own failures and passions. Of course, he is not the only one, as is clear from the many case studies. But in this book he does more than simply offer models of people who have devoted themselves to the "mucky business" of politics. He tackles common objections and concerns head-on. He also provides practical paths for others to follow suit. In its quirky, self-deprecating way, this is a book to inspire and encourage, and if a large proportion of readers get involved as a result, that has to be a good thing!
Mark Meynell, former Whitehall chaplain and author of *A Wilderness of Mirrors*

To every Christian
who believes politics is worth struggling with
rather than shrugging off –
this book is for you.

A MUCKY BUSINESS

Why Christians should get involved in politics

Tim Farron
with
Josh Price, Jo Latham, Megan Hills,
Micah Parmour and Daniel Payne

INTER-VARSITY PRESS
36 Causton Street, London SW1P 4ST, England
Email: ivp@ivpbooks.com
Website: www.ivpbooks.com

First published 2022

British Library Cataloguing-in-Publication Data
A catalogue record for this book is available from the British Library.

ISBN: 978-1-78974-444-6
eBook ISBN: 978-1-78974-445-3
Audiobook ISBN: 978-1-78974-446-0

Set in Minion Pro 10.25/13.75pt
Typeset in Great Britain by CRB Associates, Potterhanworth, Lincolnshire
Printed and bound in Great Britain by Clays Ltd, Elcograf S.p.A.

Produced on paper from sustainable sources

*Inter-Varsity Press publishes Christian books that are true to the Bible and that
communicate the gospel, develop discipleship and strengthen the church for its mission
in the world.*

*IVP originated within the Inter-Varsity Fellowship, now the Universities and Colleges
Christian Fellowship, a student movement connecting Christian Unions in universities and
colleges throughout Great Britain, and a member movement of the International Fellowship
of Evangelical Students. Website: www.uccf.org.uk. That historic association is maintained,
and all senior IVP staff and committee members subscribe to the UCCF Basis of Faith.*

MIX
Paper from
responsible sources
FSC® C018072

Contents

Contents

About the authors

Tim Farron has been MP for Westmorland and Lonsdale since 2005. He was President of the Liberal Democrats before succeeding Nick Clegg as Leader in 2015. Tim led the party through the 2016 EU referendum and the 2017 general election. He lives in the Lake District with his wife Rosie and their four children. He is a fourth-rate fell-runner, a long-suffering Blackburn Rovers supporter and a pop-music anorak.

Josh Price succeeded Megan as Tim's Parliamentary Researcher after moving to London for the Buxton Leadership Programme. Tired of political point-scoring on the news, he is determined to promote a people-focused politics of honesty, integrity and authenticity. Josh studied Geography at Newcastle University, specialising in humanitarianism, global politics and risk management, and juggling the presidency of the University Geography Society with his role as Christian Union events secretary.

Jo Latham is Faith in Public's Policy Adviser, working with Tim to encourage a better understanding of faith in the public square. She previously worked in Parliament for former MP Steve Webb, where she was involved with the Lib Dem Christian Forum and spent many hours knocking on doors for the Liberal Democrats. Jo is a primary school governor in Bedfordshire, where she lives with her husband and two daughters.

Megan Hills worked for Tim in Parliament after completing CARE's leadership programme. Having weathered hectic Brexit votes, a general election and a global pandemic, she fled to Canterbury with her husband. She worked for Jersey Road PR, seeking to reframe the perception of Christians in the media, and is now back at university, studying Speech and Language Therapy. She remains passionate about Tim-style politics: compassionate, committed and all about people.

Micah Parmour played an active role in overseas mission and church-planting in Georgia, South Carolina, prior to joining the Faith in Public team in 2021. He has a degree in Theology and a master's in International Relations. His passion is to equip Christians to think theologically about contemporary political issues, particularly in the disciplines of international relations and foreign policy.

Daniel Payne divides his week between researching, writing and generally mucking in for Faith in Public as part of his Buxton Programme Internship and serving the community with St Mary's Church Walthamstow. Daniel previously worked at a SEND school in Cornwall. He is interested to see how politics evolves from abstract ideas into practical reality.

Acknowledgments

This book has been a team effort and a work in progress ever since Tim delivered a lecture of the same name at the Keswick Convention in August 2019.

Our organization, Faith in Public, exists to encourage a better understanding of faith in the public square, and we would like to thank all those who make our work possible through donations and advice. We would particularly like to thank our directors, Mark Meynell, Sarah Latham, Alasdair Henderson and Steph Archer, and our communications team, Esther Jolliffe and Gareth Russell at Jersey Road.

Premier Christian Radio hosts and produces Tim's podcast, also called *A Mucky Business*, from which the majority of the case studies in this book have been taken. We want to thank Marcus Jones and Cara Bentley for their hard work and excellent partnership in this venture.

The authors would like to thank our families for all their support, as well as Tim's long-suffering constituency team in Westmorland and Lonsdale, and the Christians in Parliament network, all of whom have supplied fellowship, friendship and ample diary time over two decades, as we have navigated the mucky business of Westminster politics.

We also extend our appreciation to every journalist, church and student leader, fellow Christian and interested bystander who has challenged us to think more deeply about how Christianity and politics relate to each other.

Without the supportive editorial team at IVP, especially Tom Creedy, Caleb Woodbridge and Joy Tibbs, this book would never have seen the light of day. Thank you for guiding us through the process and making innumerable improvements. Any inaccuracies and controversies within are our own.

Finally, thanks to the Newcastle University Navigators of the late 1980s, without whom the title and gestation of this book would never have come about!

Introduction: Tim Farron MP

I joined the Liberal Party when I was sixteen. Two years later, just before I went off to university in Newcastle, I became a Christian. This changed my life, but it didn't stop me being heavily involved in politics. In my first year at university, I was at a Christian Union house party where a friend asked me, 'Tim, are you sure that as a Christian you should be into politics? I mean, it's a mucky business . . .'

I can't remember my reply. I suspect I didn't take his challenge as seriously as I should have. In recent years, however, that conversation has come back to me and led me to consider whether politics *is* a mucky business, and if so whether or how Christians should engage with it.

In short, my answer is that politics is absolutely a mucky business, but so is everything else, and therefore we should get involved anyway. Indeed, that is the premise of this book. We hope to persuade you that Christians should not shy away from politics; on the contrary, it should be central to our concerns and a feature of our prayers.

Just to allay your fears, this book is not written to encourage you to support a particular party or ideology!

I have been a member of the Liberal Democrats (and before that, the Liberal Party) for more than thirty-five years and a Member of Parliament (MP) for seventeen. I was Party President during the time we spent in coalition government, and Liberal Democrat Leader for two years, before stepping down because I found myself in a position where it seemed too difficult for me to lead my party well while also remaining a faithful Christian. You might think, after my experience, that I am the last person you would expect to see trying to persuade Christians to get involved in politics. But I continue to believe that politics is a world where we can do good, serve people and honour God.

I have often failed to be faithful – in some very public and other much more subtle ways. Many Christians dismiss politics out of hand as a 'mucky business'. And possibly the most frustrating and heartbreaking thing that a fellow Christian has ever said to me is that my experience was the thing that put him off getting into politics.

Others dismiss politics as not relevant to them. A sort of 'the world's all going to burn anyway' attitude that I come across frequently in Christian circles.

The authors of this book are all part of the Faith in Public team, past and present. We all know politics and Parliament from the inside and can testify that the reputation of the political world is at least partly deserved. It *is* a mucky business, but then again so is everything else on planet earth since the fall of humankind.

In this book, we will look at how we can and should engage with politics as we seek to live as faithful Christians. We want to debunk some of the myths about what a life in politics actually looks like. We also want to consider what the Bible says in relation to politics and how Christians should respond. We are in danger, as Christians, of suffering from political and cultural illiteracy just as much as secular society is accused of religious illiteracy. Not only that, but I am often surprised by how many Christians rule out even considering involvement in politics without ever really thinking it through.

It will come as no surprise that we want to persuade Christians to roll their sleeves up and get involved. We are not expecting many who read this book to become candidates or activists – but we do want to encourage all Christians to engage with politics, to care about the issues, enter into the process, understand the debates, listen and speak to politicians, and pray for those politicians and for the matters with which they grapple.

The Bible teaches us that today's leaders and politicians are flawed, that their tenure is temporary, and that their enterprises, ideologies and empires are equally flawed and temporary. But we are also taught that God uses all things for good and that his entire creation matters to him, especially the human beings he created in his own image. If they matter to him, they should matter to us.

Politics may be a mucky business, but it's a business that Christians must not fear, deride or ignore.

Part 1

WHY CHRISTIANS STEER CLEAR OF POLITICS

1

Because we are scared

I took over the leadership of the Liberal Democrats in 2015 after the former Deputy Prime Minister, Nick Clegg, stepped down. As Leader, my focus was on rebuilding a movement that had just been decimated at the ballot box following the Liberal Democrats' five years in coalition government with the Conservatives. We had gone down from fifty-seven MPs to just eight, and lost half of our councillors and a third of our party members. I would argue that no leader of any British party has ever inherited such a wasteland!

My strategy was to inspire the troops and increase our numbers, in part by picking strong and distinctive positions on Brexit, refugees, and funding for the National Health Service (NHS).

No-one sane is going to count me as a great leader, but in my two years we increased our number of MPs, increased our number of councillors and almost trebled our membership to a record size. Nevertheless I am, of course, that bloke who was a rabbit in the headlights when asked questions about what I believed – or what the Bible taught – about sex![1]

The sin that entangles most politicians, though, isn't one of those lurid ones you read about in the tabloids. It's vanity. So it's probably good that I am remembered (if I am remembered at all) for having embarrassed myself by not being able to cope with that line of questioning. Humiliation is a great antidote to vanity!

---

[1] I was questioned on numerous occasions during my leadership of the Liberal Democrats on whether I considered gay sex to be a sin, my views on abortion and other matters relating to Christian positions on personal morality. If you want to read my reflections about this time, I have written about them in my book, *A Better Ambition: Confessions of a faithful liberal* (London: SPCK, 2019).

I am a liberal. I believe everyone is equal and I believe strongly that I don't have any right to legislate to make those who aren't Christians behave as though they were. But before that, I am an orthodox Christian who – at times reluctantly – accepts the Bible's established teaching.[2]

Looking back, I'd say that the reason I struggled to give a clear answer to those questions was essentially that I'm a people-pleaser. Or at least that I chose to attempt to please or appease people rather than to play to the only audience that really matters: God, the audience of one.

Christians face two grave temptations when it comes to politics. The first is to blend in and the other is to hide. The above is a reminder that for much of my time in politics, I've been a blender-in.

Blending in comes from a desire not to offend, maybe because you are one of those nice people who doesn't want to upset people. Or maybe, for those more actively involved in politics, you are a calculating sort who doesn't want your party to lose votes. Either way, we blenders-in run the risk of losing our 'saltiness', of failing to ever make a meaningful stand for Jesus, of never sharing the gospel or living differently.

Or perhaps we do agree with actions or policies that may be socially acceptable but which, after careful study and prayerful consideration, we find still rub up against what orthodox Christian faith understands the Bible to teach. In that case we need to accept God's holy rebuke and come to terms with the possibility that our interpretation may be flawed.

Politics takes up a vast portion of my time and my headspace. I am abnormal, because for most Christians, politics is not a vocation that takes up all of their waking hours. Nevertheless, when we think

---

2 For a brief but thoughtful and thought-provoking discussion of human sexuality through a biblical lens, see Ed Shaw, *Purposeful Sexuality: A short Christian introduction* (London: IVP, 2021). For a personal and powerful story of a gay activist wrestling with these issues, see David Bennett, *A War of Loves: The unexpected story of a gay activist discovering Jesus* (Grand Rapids, MI: Zondervan, 2018).

of voting or forming opinions or even allying ourselves with a party or a cause, compromise will become part of the equation. I recall an old Liberal telling me, when I joined the party as a sixteen-year-old, that 'any Liberal who doesn't disagree with at least ten per cent of Liberal policies isn't really a Liberal'! Parties are full of people who have much in common, but those people aren't robots, and so their parties will be living coalitions of people who share a broad agenda or a central political message but don't share every single opinion. Compromise is what happens when people work together in any arena, whether it's in the office, on the football pitch or sitting around the kitchen table with the family.

I want us to consider the possibility that we can vote for a party, even join a party, when we don't agree with 100%, or even 80%, of what it stands for. We can compromise politically without compromising theologically.

In their book *Compassion (&) Conviction*, looking at faithful Christian political engagement in the United States, Justin Giboney, Michael Wear and Chris Butler helpfully explain that

> [t]wo Christians can disagree on an important policy without one or the other necessarily being unfaithful. For instance, the Bible doesn't tell us exactly how much in taxes government should collect or what the minimum wage should be. Even when the Bible does directly speak to an issue, Christians might disagree on how to apply the principle in the public square. It's a mistake to suggest that Christians should all come to the same political conclusions. However, all Christians should make those decisions from a Biblical framework.[3]

---

3 Justin Giboney, Michael Wear and Chris Butler, *Compassion (&) Conviction: The AND campaign's guide to faithful civic engagement* (Downers Grove, IL: InterVarsity Press, 2020), p. 37. The whole of ch. 3 is useful in explaining how we, as Christians, should always apply biblical principles to our political opinions, but how we can still legitimately disagree on the outworking of policy.

It is this biblical framework which helps us be alert to red flags indicating where we might be making theological compromises, sneaking around biblical standards as we seek to fit in with society's expectations. Ultimately, this framework needs to be rooted in 'love and truth, compassion and conviction, social justice and moral order'.[4] We should be compelled to apply these principles as we advocate for others, treating them with dignity in the same way that we ourselves would want to be treated. Sometimes this can present a huge challenge.

The problem with blenders-in is that they either compromise theologically and fall away from faithfully following Jesus, or else they struggle on in the faith but keep their heads down to the extent that they just don't do any good for God. That was me.

I am a repentant blender-in. I still face the temptation, but God in his mercy put me in a place where I was publicly and widely exposed as a Christian. I am no longer a rabbit in the headlights; I am instead animated roadkill! I am grateful to God that I now find myself unable to blend in any more. I am publicly known as a Christian and so there's no point in me seeking to people-please or blend in when it comes to matters relating to faith.

Those of us who are or have been blenders-in are guilty of forgetting who is really in control.

God is sovereign over all things, including the communities (online or physical) that we belong to. Nevertheless, the temptation to go along with the culture is huge because in practice we believe that the culture we are in will win out over God. When I think about my teenage children and the influences they face, I ask: 'How much pressure do they feel from those with whom they come into contact to conform to the teachings of the Bible?' And then I ask: 'How much pressure do they feel to conform to the current norms of our culture?' The honest answers to these questions have to be 'Not much' and 'A vast amount' respectively.

---

4 Giboney, Wear and Butler, *Compassion & Conviction*, p. 38.

So when we look at the current culture, airbrushing God and his laws from as much of our lives and our shared values as possible, blenders-in are in essence concluding that Christianity is defeated and that the ways of the world are ascendant. Blending in may be a conscious, subconscious or semiconscious path that we choose, because it is the easiest path for the Christian involved in politics. It is completely understandable, and it is very wrong.

Let me remind you that there was another time when it looked as though God's plan was failing, when God's people were beaten. Pontius Pilate was the ruler of Judea, representing the world's most powerful leader, Caesar of Rome. Pilate had the power of life and death over Jesus of Nazareth. He questioned Jesus, who had already been whipped, beaten, spat at and mocked and now stood before him. The religious leaders wanted Jesus dead, but they didn't have the power to have him executed. Pilate had that power, and yet he was extremely anxious: he didn't want to kill Jesus. Nevertheless, Jesus went to his death. Why? In short, because Jesus came to earth so that he could die for our sins. In which case, that is exactly what was going to happen, no matter what Pilate wanted. Because God is sovereign. The cross at Calvary looked like a place of defeat, of the ultimate defeat. Yet it wasn't; it was the place of victory. It was where the conundrum was solved – the place where mercy and justice, love and judgment met. It was the knockout victory blow as God rescued his people from sin and death. Every tragedy begins to come untrue at the cross.

Just as it was as Jesus stood before Pilate, so it is today. The cards are in reality held by the ones who look as though they've lost. God's plan has not failed. Christ has not lost. So why behave as if he has?

We are called, as every generation of Christians is, to love the people in the world, to focus on repenting for our own sins rather than pointing out the sins of others, but at the same time, not to blend in with the culture and behave as though God is OK with everything in it, because we know that he isn't.

We need to resist the temptation to hide away, too. Politics is a mucky business, in part because our culture is full of expressions of the rejection of God's laws. It often feels as if the opinion-formers out there have mostly rejected Christ, his claims and his teaching, and seem to be determined to lead others to the same conclusions. It is so much safer, isn't it, to zip ourselves into a little Christian bubble and stay there until judgment day. Or at least to take the 'safety first' option and protect ourselves from becoming sullied and impure. Hiding away, then, is what so many Christians do, consciously or otherwise.

The central purpose of this book is to help Christians think about politics and to engage with current affairs. We are not trying to persuade readers that they must stand for Parliament (although we would rejoice if this book helped you decide to)! We simply want more Christians to think about, pray about, understand and engage with the political world. So if you recognize that you are a hider, don't fear that I'm telling you that you must now become an MP! Maybe that might persuade some of you to unzip your bubbles and tiptoe outside; it's not as frightening as all that . . .

I encounter a high degree of naivety about politics among some Christians, and to some degree that seems to be due to this tendency to hide, to focus on eternity while blotting out the grottiness of the world around us.

It is comfortable and safe in the Christian bubble, and while we must meet together, pray together, worship together, support one another in our needs and our weaknesses, and hear the teaching of the Word together, we are not meant to stay entirely inside that bubble.

I say this for two reasons. One is about evangelism and the other is about service.

In Luke 9 and 10, Jesus sends out his followers as 'workers into his harvest field . . . like lambs among wolves' (Luke 10:2–3). We too are called to go out into the world and deliver the good news about

Jesus. That means building relationships with people who are not Christians, otherwise we won't have that opportunity. Or if we do get that opportunity we won't really understand the language of the society into which we wish to speak. In Acts 17, Paul was taken before the Areopagus in Athens – a council of the city's leaders and thinkers – and spoke to them in their 'language'. These were Gentiles, not Jews. He talked to them about the 'unknown God' that they worshipped, and alluded to some of their cultural references (v. 28: 'As some of your own poets have said . . .'). He understood Athenian society and used that understanding to explain Christ in a way that made sense to them.

Our calling to engage with the world of politics and current affairs goes beyond the Great Commission to share the gospel and win souls for Christ. We are also called by God to 'seek the peace and prosperity of the city to which I have carried you into exile. Pray to the LORD for it, because if it prospers, you too will prosper' (Jeremiah 29:7). Or, in the words of the English Standard Version (ESV), '. . . in its welfare you will find your welfare'. This means that we are called to seek the good of the society in which we have been placed, not to distance ourselves from that culture or its people. Jeremiah was talking of a place of exile and a nation that had done a great wrong to God's people – so we aren't given much latitude here. Even if the society you are in is strongly opposed to you, you are actively to seek the good of those around you.

In the Gospels, we read of how Jesus commissioned the twelve disciples to 'proclaim the kingdom of God *and* to heal those who were ill' (Luke 9:2, my emphasis). Evangelism and service go hand in hand.

In the biblical accounts of the lives of Daniel and Joseph, we see this theme expanded. Joseph (Genesis 37 – 46) becomes Pharaoh's chief minister, acting on behalf of one who had enslaved him and imprisoned him, and for a regime that would over time enslave the entire nation of Israel and subject the people to unspeakable acts of violence and persecution. Yet God does not call Joseph to sabotage or sulk; he calls him to serve.

Daniel likewise rises to the highest levels in government, serving under a king who had occupied his country and stolen him and his friends from their families and taken them into slavery. Daniel is, of course, famously called to make a death-defying stand: he must either deny his God, or else worship him and face execution (Daniel 6). Daniel chose to worship God and face the consequences – his ordeal in the lions' den. Yet, before this, Daniel had served in Babylon for many decades, gaining greater and greater responsibility and finally occupying a place at the top of government without – apparently – having to stand out in such a way that martyrdom became an option.

Maybe I am reading too much into the years of Daniel's life about which the Bible is silent, but perhaps it is fair to conclude that the Bible is silent about those years because they were relatively un-eventful. It seems that Daniel did not face persecution or a dramatic test on a scale of the lions' den for most of his time in office. May we assume, then, that for most of our time, if we serve in the alien land that is worldly politics, we can expect to do so quietly and without drama? Martyrdom is a noble calling, but it is surely not one that anyone should actively seek. Joseph and Daniel didn't seek it, and neither should we. We should dutifully serve.

There are times in my own experience when I know that the Bible says something that the company I am in – or the journalist who is interviewing me – would consider to be outrageous or wrong. I often feel a huge temptation to go headlong into dealing with the hot-button issue in question, but I am not duty-bound to do so! The fact that God says to those who do not yet believe, 'You are not your own, you owe everything to me,' is countercultural and radical enough without having to add insult to injury. Believe me, to the non-Christian, the most offensive thing about Christianity is not the specific sins that receive so much attention, but rather the funda-mental concept of there actually being a God to whom we are accountable. It is amazing how angry people can get about a God that they say they don't believe in.

I have learned – maybe a little later than I could have done – that we don't have to blurt out everything the Bible says about the hot topic of the day to be a faithful Christian. We are called to be wise and appropriate in how we share the gospel and to live good and quiet lives. Even if we feel the eyes of suspicion upon us from a society that thinks about sex (to pick a completely random example) very differently from us, we are not called to play other people's games and give them the confrontation they desire. Like Daniel, our faithfulness *might* show itself in a moment that feels like a lions' den, but also, like Daniel, it might be shown in the dutiful quiet service that goes unreported and unseen, except by God, the one whose opinion matters most.

When Jesus was asked vexatious questions by the Pharisees, Sadducees or other accusers, he often gave oblique answers, or at least an answer that the questioner wasn't bargaining for. If a politician gave the same kind of answers as those offered by Jesus, we might call him or her 'slippery'. But Jesus was right to answer in those ways, first because he knew that his questioners needed to know the answer to questions they weren't asking, and second, because we are not obliged to go jumping with both feet into every predictable trap that the devil or the world sets us. Perhaps following Jesus is more political than we like to think!

This sounds as if we need to be wary of the world, and to a degree we do. We must only be wary, though, in order to persevere in our faith in Christ and so be able to lead others to believe in him. You *may* end up among the people to such an extent that you are blessed with the opportunity to stand on a podium and make the altar call, but mostly our evangelism will be personal; it often comes out of earning respect from people who see us serving in a way which is loving, humble and sacrificial, and which earns us the right to be heard among the most ungodly of people. Just as the lives of Daniel and Joseph are filled with years of service, so should ours be, as we echo the example of our servant king, Jesus.

To follow Christ is to follow his example, and his example was one of intense compassion for people everywhere. In Matthew 9:36, we read that Jesus 'had compassion on them, because they were harassed and helpless'. I think that we are compelled to care for people's physical needs as well as their spiritual needs. James tells us that 'if anyone . . . knows the good they ought to do and doesn't do it, it is sin for them' (James 4:17). When we live in a society where we see poverty, homelessness or injustice, or see people whose lives are miserable and we know we could do something to make those lives better, I believe that it is sinful when we do not roll our sleeves up and do something to help.

That doesn't mean that we are compelled to follow a particular ideology; nor does it compel us to rush out, join a party and stand for Parliament. It does, however, mean that if we follow Jesus, we shouldn't be hermits when it comes to politics. We should seek to understand politics, and pray for and have a heart for those who are our leaders locally and nationally. We don't need to agree with them to love them. Likewise, we should care deeply about the welfare of those who are affected by political decisions, including those who are at the sharp end of injustice of all kinds.

If we can use overseas mission as an analogy here, we might reflect that Christian missionaries are greatly aided in sharing the gospel if they can speak the local language – but that speaking and understanding the local language does not mean they have to accept the local gods! We saw this above, in Paul's engagement with the Athenians at the Areopagus. For us, this means that we can and should seek to understand our culture, and love the people who are immersed in it, while not accepting its rightness before God. That way, we may be able to level with the people to whom we want to witness, with at least a working understanding of where they are coming from.

This is a fallen world, and all the people in it are fallen too – including us. Even so, I am not sure we win a hearing for the gospel if all we ever do is speak about people's lives, and about our society as a whole, in a way that suggests we find them and it despicable! First-century Judea was full of deeply sinful practices, yet Jesus did not go around looking down his nose at the people of that society, treating them with a kind of contemptuous disgust; nor did he allow others to easily depict him that way. He was utterly holy *and* utterly involved. We follow the one who is utterly holy, and we need to learn from Jesus how to love the people who don't love him.

Let me give you an example of what not to do!

In 2018, I was due to speak at a large Christian event in Manchester. I was going to be interviewed on the stage by my pastor on the matter of living for Jesus in the public eye. About four hundred people were expected to attend. I was really looking forward to it.

Forty-eight hours before the event, I endured one of those delightful eruptions of Twitter fury. The cause was the discovery of a flyer that had been distributed to some churches in Manchester ahead of this event. I hadn't seen it in advance, but it listed the speakers for the day and it carried a bit of text that was not all that wise. It talked about the challenges to Christianity of 'mass immigration and the gay lobby'. Now, if that statement sounds perfectly reasonable to you, let me explain why it struck such an offensive chord with so many people.

First, immigration in my view is a very good thing. How much worse would our preparedness for coronavirus have been without the thousands of non-UK NHS staff? Also, a much greater proportion of migrants to this country have an active Christian faith than is the case among those who are already here. Second, the phrase 'the gay lobby' implies nefarious conspiracy and is deliberately demeaning. Put simply, referring to 'mass immigration' and the 'gay lobby' was a tone-deaf thing to do. The derogatory language heightened a sense of 'us versus them' that can sometimes arise when Christians feel threatened by the rest of society, but it simply repels those to whom we should be holding out the gospel, before they even get as far as considering the claims of Christ. If we are seeking to understand our culture and care for our people then we must aim to live holy lives in obedience to Christ, but we should not use language that unnecessarily inflames, offends or gives others an excuse to ignore the gospel.

In the end, the only thing I could do was withdraw from that event, which was a terrible shame. I spoke to some of those from our church who attended, and they were really encouraged and blessed by it, but the lack of cultural literacy on that flyer was a problem.

We need to understand how we are heard. The more we hide away, the less we will have an accurate sense of how our culture speaks and how our culture hears.

So what should we do? Well, don't blend in and don't hide away. Simple! Be friends with non-Christians, care about their lives, and seek to understand the culture and the motives behind their opinions and choices. At the same time, we should discipline ourselves to spend time with Christian friends, keep our roots in good soil and bear fruit. But if we don't engage in the politics of the world and the results of the decisions that politicians make, then we may bear fruit that is never shared.

Case study: Kate Forbes, Member of the Scottish Parliament (MSP)

Kate Forbes' rise to become Scotland's Finance and Economy Minister was unexpected and dizzying in its speed. Raised the daughter of Christian missionaries in India and Scotland, she came to Christ as an inquisitive child, seeing that he was the only constant in a childhood of completely different countries and cultures and a world of shifting sands. From the minute Kate was thrown into a higher-profile position in the devolved Scottish government for the Scottish Nationalist Party (SNP), she has been upfront and blunt about her faith. She has answered with rare clarity and boldness when asked questions in secular news media about what she believes. She told Nick Robinson on the BBC's Political Thinking podcast:

> To be straight, I believe in the person of Jesus Christ. I believe that he died for me, he saved me and that my calling is to serve and to love him and to serve and love my neighbours with all my heart and soul and mind and strength. So that for me is essential to my being. Politics will pass – I am a person before I was a politician, and that person will continue to believe that I am made in the image of God.[5]

Kate is part of the Free Church of Scotland – a conservative evangelical tradition. The stark contrast on some issues between this church's views and the SNP's views, and even the general culture of politics, might seem to create a gap that is difficult to bridge. But she is clear on how she addresses scepticism and difficult questions.

'The first step is to know what you believe and why.' This takes time and patience. It takes time to mature in our understanding of faith and why we trust in Jesus. It takes a commitment to studying the Bible, perhaps listening to good teaching, and weighing up what you really believe. Kate explains: 'It's a lot easier to defend a position that you inherently believe rather than defending a position that you just think Christians should hold.'

---

5 <www.bbc.co.uk/programmes/p09j7xy1> (accessed 29 June 2022).

Can you articulate what you really believe about Jesus and the claims he made? How and why does that affect the entirety of our lives – our behaviour, our attitudes, and yes, our politics? We trust in him, and that changes everything. As 1 Peter 3:15 (ESV) says: 'in your hearts honour Christ the Lord as holy, always being prepared to make a defence to anyone who asks you for a reason for the hope that is in you; yet do it with gentleness and respect.'

Kate continues: 'The second thing is, you've got to figure out how to build a bridge to your listeners … It's asking: What relevance does the gospel have to the twenty-first-century UK? How would you sit next to somebody on a train and explain why you believe what you believe, because if it doesn't resonate with them, then it's not going to make sense on a podcast or in a media interview. What is the world out there hearing when we speak? You've got to make sure they're hearing what you intend to say, rather than hearing something because of all the baggage and filtering that goes on with Christian views.'

Kate's experience shows that an understanding of how our culture thinks is crucial to be able to give a good account of the gospel. This also takes time and patience! We must listen to our friends and neighbours. Kate is the first to confess she has got this wrong many times: 'It takes practice … I have got things wrong in town halls, I've got things wrong in media interviews, I've got things wrong with just speaking to friends and family.'

Kate's high position in the SNP, a party of diverse political and religious views spanning from militant secularists to orthodox Christians, seems very likely to continue upwards. Kate says Christians should be 'ambitious for excellence', not to get praise, 'but because we have all been given a gift, and we'll all give an account for how we use those gifts'. No doubt, Kate is one to watch.

2

Because we believe things aren't what they used to be

There is a UK TV programme called *It Was Alright in the 70s* in which a bunch of zeitgeisty types sit around watching TV clips from before they were born.[1] The zeitgeisty types then either laugh or explode with outrage at the things they see. Some of the stuff is genuinely outrageous, such as casual violence against women, 'comedy' racism and ugly homophobic abuse. I am pretty sure that much of that stuff was unacceptable in the 1970s too. The presenters often also express incredulity at naive depictions of domesticity, and of outmoded leisure pursuits and patterns of work. There are tuts, gasps and sniggers.

Here's a confident prediction. In forty-five years' time, the zeitgeisty types of the 2060s will look back at the culture in our age. They will be horrified at some aspects of our society, and they will find other things that we do and think utterly hilarious.

I am not certain which parts of our culture they will mock or deride, but you can be sure they will find something.

This is a book written by Christians, and we are therefore under some kind of unwritten obligation to quote C. S. Lewis from time to time. The term 'snobbery of chronology' was first deployed by Lewis in his book *Surprised by Joy*, although he credits his friend Owen Barfield with having introduced him to the concept. The snobbery of chronology is the assumption that our age is better than yesteryear and that there is a sort of linear historical trajectory which means

---

1 See, for example, series 2, episode 1: <www.youtube.com/watch?v=3_s5mdTUivU> (accessed 29 June 2022).

that humanity gets better with each generation – the best of all (for now) being the generation that *we* belong to.

Lewis describes chronological snobbery as

the uncritical acceptance of the intellectual climate common to our own age and the assumption that whatever has gone out of date is on that account discredited. You must find out why it went out of date. Was it ever refuted and if so by whom, where and how conclusively? Or did it merely die away as fashions do?[2]

In other words, it's just patronizing and empty-headed to assume that the present is automatically superior to the past. The opposite, by the way, is also true.

Many conservative-minded people, including some in the church, slip into reverse chronological snobbery. They fall for the nonsense (and it *is* nonsense) that yesterday is automatically better than today. 'Make America Great Again' (MAGA), and the equivalent slogans in Western Europe, play on the latent belief in the back of our minds that there was once a golden age and that we must rediscover it. It might be the 1950s or the 1980s . . . or the Blair years . . . before we lost the British Empire, before we left Europe . . . when the music was better . . . and so on and so forth. But we are just as likely to fall for the lure of looking back to a golden age as we are to be seduced by the idea that the current age is superior to those that have gone before.

We need to understand very clearly that, since the fall of human-kind, there has never been a golden age. Every age is tainted by the errors and evils of the flawed people who lived then and especially the flawed people who ruled then. Yesterday only seems better to us because we were younger!

Some things about today are better than yesterday, and some things are worse. In the UK, we now have the highest percentage of

2   C. S. Lewis, *Surprised by Joy* (London: Collins, 2012), p. 241.

people surviving a diagnosis of cancer . . . and yet we have the largest number of people dying as a result of suicide. Slavery in the West is abolished . . . and yet it exists behind closed doors in every city in the UK. We have freedom to live as we choose, marry whom we choose and be divorced from that person as we choose . . . and yet we have the financial hardship and mental health crises that go hand in hand with relationship breakdown, especially when children are involved.

Are we going forwards or are we going backwards?

We can only answer that question if there is an objective standard to measure against. So which standard would you pick? If it's the standard of the zeitgeisty types, it will be skewed to the standards and values that seem right today . . . and if it's the MAGA types it will be skewed to the standards and values that they assume were the norm back in the golden age – in which case we are snookered. Unless there really *are* some common values, something objective that we can measure our society against.

The claim of Christianity is that not only is God eternal but his values and his laws are too.

That we take a 'two-thousand-year-old book' seriously is of course a source of ridicule for many. (In fact, much of the Bible is a good deal older than that.[3]) But here's a thought. The Sermon on the Mount was delivered in around AD 29. Since then, thousands of bright new philosophies, ideologies and political leaders have arisen, have had their moment and have now gone. Jesus' words have survived. Most of the inspiring leaders we follow today will be dead and discredited in a hundred years' time. The evidence of the last twenty centuries is that Christianity will continue.

Christianity jars with every culture. If it's not being dismissed for being out of date, then it's subversive instead, or else it's austere, or maybe permissive. There is no good reason to reject Jesus, but there's no shortage of reasons either. You won't need to look far to find one.

---

3 See Amy Orr-Ewing, *Why Trust the Bible? Answers to 10 tough questions*, rev. edn (London: IVP, 2020), for more in-depth analysis of this point.

Christianity is countercultural today because it declares that we are not our own gods; that our ultimate aim in life is not to be 'true to ourselves' and live in orbit around our feelings and desires; it is to be humble before the real God and to live in orbit around him. This is offensive to today's cultural narrative, which states that 'religion' is designed by elites simply to control and oppress people, and to take away the agency of individuals to create their own identities as they see fit. In previous generations, Christianity rubbed up against the culture of the day slightly differently regarding bloodthirsty militarism, religious legalism or the racist degradation of slavery, to name just three major issues.

If you are a Christian, then, you know that it is your duty to love your neighbour. You also know that every human being is made in the image of God, which means that every one of us possesses a dignity and an equality that far exceeds that of any secular world view. Sure, many belief systems will tell us that all people are equal. But equal at what level? Equally the result of a cosmological and biological accident? Equal because of some arbitrary assumption of the philosophy that we currently subscribe to, but which might be deemed outdated soon?

Here's the real problem for the non–Christian who wants to dismiss Christianity and Christian values as out of date, and it's a problem for Christians too: I don't want to sound mean but it is *your* values that have no lasting validity. Maybe you believe in the innate value of every human being; maybe you believe in equality; maybe you believe that the exploitation of the powerless by the powerful is wrong. Good for you; so do I. But without God, I'm afraid that these values are arbitrary and have no call on the next generation.

On what basis do you draw those conclusions? Because they feel right? Christianity tells us that those values feel right because God put them in our hearts. In Romans 2:15, Paul claims the promise that God made to the people of Israel in Jeremiah 31:33 – that he has 'put his law in [our] minds and [written] it on [our] hearts'. But if we're wrong, if there is no God, then those values are just made-up fashions of the age. They are pleasant notions, but they have no call on anyone. In other words, those notions and values are primed and ready to go out of date at some point. Listen to the language of some today who think it is alright for governments to break international law, for journalists to be barred from writing what they think, for comedians to be censored for satire . . . and you will see that the values that post-war liberal democracies have bequeathed to us – wonderful though they may be – seem to be heading out of fashion at an alarming rate.

Those values of justice, equality and fairness, those qualities of humility, kindness, patience, faithfulness, truthfulness . . . all of them are based on the understanding that humans are made in the image of God. They underpin our liberal democracies, and they arise from our Judeo-Christian heritage.[4] In *Inventing the Individual*, historian Larry Siedentop suggests it was Paul's teachings that first gave rise to the radical idea that the sacrificial love of Jesus Christ was open to every single individual, whether Jew or Gentile, slave or free, male or female (Galatians 3:28):

> Paul's conception of the Christ overturns the assumption on which ancient thinking had hitherto rested, the assumption of natural inequality. Instead, Paul wagers on human equality . . . [and] a moral agency potentially available to each and everyone, that is, to individuals. This 'universal' freedom, with its moral implications, was utterly different from the freedom enjoyed by the privileged class of citizens in the polis.[5]

Of course, many people strongly believe in these values and at the same time have no faith in Christ, but I would put this to them: those

---

4   For an excellent overview of the Christian roots of many of the values we take for granted in our society, see Glen Scrivener's *The Air We Breathe: How we all came to believe in freedom, kindness, progress, and equality* (Surrey: The Good Book Company, 2022).

5   Larry Siedentop, *Inventing the Individual: The origins of Western liberalism* (Milton Keynes: Penguin, 2014), p. 60.

values and qualities will go out of date if they have no root in an eternal source. If they have no eternal source, then they are at the mercy of the next emerging world view. 'The rule of law? Ha! It was alright in the 2020s . . .'

Christianity has a uniquely high view of humanity because the Bible teaches that we are the apex of creation, made just 'a little lower than the angels' (Psalm 8:5), but this accurate, lofty view of human beings can become distorted into a tendency to think that humans are capable of perfection, that technological progress is a sign of our continued moral improvement. Christians need to keep their feet on the ground. In the varying cultures of every age, in the economics, the society, the thinking of every generation, there will be moral failure because they are all shaped by human moral failures like you and me.

Few things lift my spirits and inspire me more than NASA's Apollo programme; the ambition, the courage, the audacity, the ingenuity and the jaw-dropping success of it fill me with awe. I know how tempting it can be to see humanity making progress and conclude: 'If we can do that, then just think what else we can do!' I'd love to go to Cape Canaveral and see the relics of the Apollo missions. I have, however, been to Auschwitz and seen the relics of something quite different. The shorn hair, the toys, the prosthetic limbs taken from children, women and men who were sent to their death in the gas chambers. If we can do that, then just think what else we could do.

So let's not fall into the trap of judging today by a lower standard than yesterday . . . or indeed judging yesterday by a lower standard than today. As Christians, we should be conscious most of all of our own sin, of our own fallenness. Let's replace our tendency to chronological snobbery with an attempt at chronological honesty.

That doesn't mean that we give the past a free pass. By all means, let us have a conversation about whether or not to take down statues and monuments to people of significance in ages past if that is consistent with a repentance of our own wrongs; if that is consistent with a humble desire to live faithfully in this age. Let us not, however, delude ourselves that by pointing the finger at the baddies of the past and emptying their plinths, we can avoid judgment for our own moral failures. We will see our own moral failures far less clearly than those of the people whose statues we tear down, because our moral failures do not jar with the culture of today; indeed they are likely to be integral to the culture of today. The snobbery of chronology must give way to a humility and respect for people in all ages, and we can only judge the goodness or badness of those cultures against the same eternal standard that, by definition, can never go out of date.

A final word on this. When I was at university I would often get involved in lengthy discussions – usually in the Union bar – with far-left socialists, Marxists, Trotskyists ... even the odd Maoist. I enjoyed those discussions; most of them were heated but good-natured and respectful. You see, I really admired those people. I admired the neat and orderly view they had of society, and I agreed with many of their assessments of what was wrong even if I couldn't agree with their conclusions as to how to put things right. But I also felt sorry for them because they were doomed to disappointment. If you believe that your politics can perfect people's lives, you can only fail and become weighed down by that failure, always at least one more steep ridge away from seeing the top of the mountain.

But for me, as someone who believes that perfection will surely elude us in this life, I know that while I wait for Jesus to either return or call me home, I can still do some good. I can have peace knowing that my contribution to making my part of the world a bit fairer, a bit kinder, a bit better governed, is a worthwhile exercise. It is a service to the perfect God who gave me that work to do, and it is a service to my neighbours. Politics then becomes a source of satisfaction, a noble endeavour where I can do some good in an evil time. As Christians, we must never indulge in the distortion that is the snobbery of chronology, because the only age in which we can actively have influence is the one the Lord has put us in. Today.

Case study: Carla Lockhart MP

The central Bible verse of Carla Lockhart's political career has been Esther 4:14:

> For if you remain silent at this time, relief and deliverance for the Jews will arise from another place, but you and your father's family will perish. And who knows but that you have come to your royal position for such a time as this?

In context, the verse is part of a rebuke and challenge to Esther when she found herself in her new position of influence in the royal courts. The same was true for Carla when she won her Northern Irish seat of Upper Bann in 2019. She now had a voice and a position of influence. How would she use it for the time God had put her there for?

There is one burning issue on Carla's heart: 'I genuinely believe that I am in Parliament for such a time as this – particularly on issues such as abortion.' The motivation is a familiar biblical one: 'For me, I'm young, I'm female. This is what keeps me in politics, because I firmly believe I need to be a voice for the voiceless.'

The voiceless she speaks of are the unborn. Carla says that currently the tone of the abortion debate so often 'grieves me', and that the baby in the womb should be humanized and thought of as a person. But she reserves her most powerful challenge for Christians and the church. Perhaps, for some of us, the simple part is telling what Christians believe about abortion. The hard bit, practically, is allowing for an alternative, both in legislation and in life.

'We need to step out of our comfort zone . . . and actually come alongside these people who find themselves in a situation where they feel they actually can't continue the pregnancy and we need to show real, practical Christianity,' says Carla. In politics then, 'yes, it's important that the legislative framework is life-affirming', but this cannot just stop at abortion law if the lives of both mother and child really do matter. The two-child cap on child benefit, for example, 'plunges people into financial difficulty'; similarly, she argues that there should be more childcare available for families who worry they can't afford it.

For such a time as this. Not to bring back the past. Not to be remembered and glorified into the future. But to use this time she has been allotted now to do what she can. *For such a time as this.*

3

Because we don't speak the language

The job of the evangelist sounded so much easier a century ago. The majority of people in Britain went to church; it was a chore for most of them, but they went.[1] All you needed to do was preach the gospel at them, and some of those sitting in the pews would experience a personal epiphany, respond, and accept the offer of eternal life by grace through faith in the Lord Jesus Christ.

The ones who didn't respond and put their trust in Christ nevertheless knew their Bible stories and they probably felt that their identity was in part Christian. They understood roughly what the commandments were and what 'being a Christian' looked like.

Forty years ago, things had changed. Fewer people in the UK went to church, but their parents or grandparents probably had attended and so people still tended to know the Bible stories. They vaguely believed in the existence of a god and assumed that god to be the one referred to in the Bible. Some may have been to Sunday school. Up until the 1970s, if you did Religious Education at school, it will mostly have focused on Christian teaching; indeed, at primary school the lesson was sometimes still called 'Scripture'.

As recently as the 1980s, then, Christian teaching, values and observance were knitted into the culture of the UK. As a result,

---

1 The 1851 census recorded a churchgoing population of 10.5 million on Sunday, 30 March 1851, out of a population of just under 18 million: <www.brin.ac.uk/figures/churches-and-churchgoers/census-1851-england-and-wales> (accessed 29 June 2022); <https://search.findmypast.co.uk/search-world-records/1851-england-wales-and-scotland-census> (accessed 29 June 2022).

Christianity wouldn't have seemed all that alien to the average person, even in a society where many or most people did not attend church.

Fast-forward to the 2020s and the change has been huge. The British Social Attitudes survey showed that in 1983, 66% of British people considered themselves to be 'Christian', while 31% stated that they had no religion. By 2018, though, a majority of respondents to the question on religious identity said that they followed no religion (52%), with the number of self-identifying Christians having plummeted to 38%.[2]

The biggest decline seems to have been among those declaring affiliation to the Church of England – falling from 40% of the population in 1983 to just 12% in 2018. Other denominations had also lost adherents, with Catholic identification down from 10% to 7% and Presbyterians and Methodists falling from 5% and 4%, respectively, down to just 1% each.[3]

There was one indicator of Christian growth, however, and that was among those who identified as Christian with *no* denomination, whose numbers rose from 3% of the UK population in 1983 to 13% in 2018.[4] Who are those people? Well, they may include some who see themselves as culturally Christian but who don't attend church or have a particularly deep faith commitment. However, it seems likely that many are those who belong to independent 'free' churches, most of which are evangelical and 'reformed' in their theology. These are the churches that often meet in school halls, community centres or even people's homes rather than owning their own church buildings. In this group, the real numerical growth is in the black-majority churches. The London Church Census found that two new London churches opened every week between 2005 and 2012. Two thirds of these were Pentecostal black-majority churches, and a

2 <https://bsa.natcen.ac.uk/media/39293/1_bsa36_religion.pdf> (accessed 29 June 2022).
3 <https://bsa.natcen.ac.uk/media/39293/1_bsa36_religion.pdf> (accessed 29 June 2022).
4 <https://bsa.natcen.ac.uk/media/39293/1_bsa36_religion.pdf> (accessed 29 June 2022).

third catered for a particular language or ethnic group.[5] A 2014 study found 240 black-majority churches in the London Borough of Southwark alone, believed to be 'the greatest concentration of African Christianity in the world outside Africa'.[6]

The growth of these churches has therefore done little to prevent the decline in the use of the traditional parish church. The closure and repurposing of those buildings continues to be a very visible sign of Christian retreat from the life of the wider community, but it may hide a reality of a growing movement of gospel-believing churches full of beautiful people who meet in ugly buildings!

The growth in the UK of those Christian churches, full of passion for gospel truth and bursting with life – yet meeting in more mundane settings – is reminiscent of the nature of church life for Christians in those parts of the world where the faith is very clearly growing hugely and rapidly. In China or Iran, for instance, much of the church meets in informal and often very small settings, given the presence of sinister scrutiny and persecution for those who declare their Christian faith. Yet, it is in those countries where hardship and persecution are present that Christianity appears to be flourishing. No-one wishes for poverty and persecution, but there is something about those pressures that seem to go hand in hand with Christian growth.

In John 6:68, Peter's words, spoken in response to Jesus' enquiry as to whether Peter and the other disciples would join those who were deserting him, strike a chord with many of us: 'Lord, to whom shall we go? You have the words of eternal life.' There is a desperation in what Peter says. In effect it is: 'I've got nowhere else to go, Lord. You are my only hope.' It strikes a chord because there is a desperation in the heart of every believer. If we have concluded that the gospel is

---

5 <www.eauk.org/church/one-people-commission/stories/black-and-ethnic-christians-lead-london-church-growth.cfm> (accessed 29 June 2022).

6 <https://blogs.lse.ac.uk/religionglobalsociety/2016/12/how-are-black-majority-churches-growing-in-the-uk-a-london-borough-case-study> (accessed 29 June 2022).

true, we know we have nowhere else to turn and so we cling to Jesus. Maybe the more comfortable and 'free' we are, the less our desperation is apparent to us?

Christianity is assumed to be a Western religion, the faith of the developed world. It isn't any more.

The Centre for the Study of Global Christianity estimates that in 1900 Christians in the Global North outnumbered those in the Global South by more than four to one. The total number of believers was thought to be just short of 560 million at that point.

Dramatically, by 2021 the tables had turned. The number of Christians in the Global South now exceeds those in the Global North by more than two to one, with the total number of Christians on the planet put at more than 2.5 billion.[7]

Christianity has not declined, but the geographical distribution of believers has shifted radically.

Confusingly, the Global North is often referred to as 'the West', or 'the developed world', but these definitions largely describe the same group of nations – those that are European either in their location or their heritage.

One theory is that as the West has become more educated, less deferential and more rational, religion has declined. The assumption is that people in the 'developing world' haven't yet 'caught up with us' when it comes to rational thought, but as they do, religion in general and Christianity in particular will die out globally. This is horrifically patronizing, culturally imperialist, chronologically snobbish . . . and quite obviously wrong.

Those celebrating the decline of Christianity in the West would be wise to look over their shoulders and take note of the more general decline in the power and significance of the 'West' itself, as the developing powers grow and gain ascendancy. It seems likely that

---

7   Aaron Earls, '7 surprising trends in global Christianity', Lifeway Research, 11 June 2019: <https://research.lifeway.com/2019/06/11/7-surprising-trends-in-global-christianity-in-2019> (accessed 29 June 2022).

Western values, far from slowly but surely seeping into the cultures of the developing world, are actually under threat due to the steady evaporation of Western leadership of global affairs.

We would need another chapter, or indeed another book, to look at the extent to which those two trends are connected. Tom Holland points out, in his magisterial tome *Dominion*, that Christianity is the 'single most transformative development in Western history'.[8] Holland demonstrates that it is no coincidence that the West has been *both* Christian *and* the birthplace of liberal democracy. One led to the other. 'To live in a Western country', he says, 'is to live in a society still utterly saturated by Christian concepts and assumptions.'[9] As theologian Oliver O'Donovan says, Western liberal democracy bears the crater marks of the gospel.[10]

Many will see no almighty hand in this at all, but even so, it seems self-evident that a society which rejects the faith that spawned the values on which it was built might then see its very structure begin to decline and even dissolve.

What is surely beyond doubt is the fact that Western societies now include a large majority of people who have little or no knowledge of religion in general and of Christianity in particular. For Baby Boomers and for Generation X, Christianity was the faith of their parents, but for Millennials and Generation Z, Christianity is instead the faith of a small number of people they don't know, don't understand and probably don't like.

If Christianity is true, then it means you aren't in charge of how you should live your life, but instead you are subject to another, and

---

8   Tom Holland, *Dominion: The making of the Western mind* (Boston: Little, Brown, 2019), p. xxv.
9   Holland, *Dominion*, p. xxv.
10 Oliver O'Donovan, *The Desire of the Nations: Rediscovering the roots of political theology* (Cambridge: Cambridge University Press, 1996), p. 212, quoted in James K. A. Smith, *Awaiting the King: Reforming public theology* (Grand Rapids, MI: Baker Academic, 2017), p. 98: 'Like the surface of a planet pocked with craters by the bombardment it receives from space, the governments of the passing age show the impact of Christ's dawning glory.'

if your opinions over how to live your life clash with the opinions of God then you are wrong and he is right.

Let's not pretend that this has ever been an attractive position in any society.

Yet, perhaps in the past the cultural affinity people had towards the church, and the fact that they knew Christians in their own families, meant they were more tolerant and understanding of those who accepted that radical world view.

Today, if you choose to live frugally and give away 'excess' funds, forgo career advancement in order to care for and serve others, forgive people who do or say horrible things to you, deny yourself sexually, and refrain from watching or reading things that you might otherwise enjoy, you may well be considered odd and joyless.

Most people will consider you to be unreasonable if you think it is important to be in church on a Sunday and not have to work on that day, to be free to raise your children to believe in Christ, and to not have to endure hearing Jesus' name glibly used as a swearword in TV dramas.

That these things are considered anachronistic or even problematic by significant chunks of our contemporaries tells us a lot about the lack of religious literacy in Western societies. Religious observance has become something that is beyond the experience of most people. As a result, the majority simply don't understand the minority who believe.

Let's go to some even more controversial positions. To hold that life begins at conception, not just because you believe that God 'knitted you together in your mother's womb' (see Psalm 139:13) and accept that life at every stage is precious, but simply because it's a reasonable position irrespective of one's faith, is no longer widely understood or tolerated. Neither is it accepted that a person can reasonably hold that marriage should be between one woman and one man, publicly declared and for life. Even those who hold that belief while nevertheless accepting a legal right for people to make different choices are considered to be unpleasant or even dangerous.

Of course, Christians are legally free to believe such things, for now . . . but very few people in our society would accept that those beliefs are reasonable.

Someone might strongly disagree with the concept of Scottish independence, the UK's exit from the European Union (EU), or Irish unification, yet still accept that the alternative point of view is one that is reasonable to hold and doesn't necessarily make the holder a weird or bad person.

Maybe that is because, however irritating we might find opposing views on such emotive subjects, we know many people who hold those views and we therefore understand them even if we don't like them. The fading of Christianity from the experience of most people in the West means that they increasingly don't understand what underpins such 'unreasonable' views on sex, life, death, Sundays and swearing.

Let's call a spade a spade: Western societies have morphed into arrogance, foolishness and discrimination when it comes to their interaction with Christians. This is due to a fundamental ignorance about what motivates Christians. Is it the fault of those with no faith background that they have little experience of Christians, and therefore have little sympathy for what we believe and little concern for why we believe it? No, not entirely. Since most people have grown up in a society where Christianity is alien to them, they don't speak the language and so why should they understand? And anyway, it all feels so weird, restrictive and unattractive – why would they *want* to understand? Perhaps we need to challenge non-believers to apply society's stated commitment to diversity and equality in reality, and not just where it is convenient? I would suggest that those who put their fingers in their ears and refuse to consider whether it is reasonable to have a world view influenced by a religious faith have accidentally slipped into bigotry.

I've done my best to state these things bluntly without seeming to complain, because Christians are called to turn the other cheek. It is neither godly nor a 'good look' for us to whine about such developments. If God is for us, who can be against us? Despite these developments in Western culture, they are nothing for Christians to worry about. Instead, we should be encouraged by the worldwide growth of the church, by the knowledge that our lives are – as they should be – countercultural, and by the fact that we have the opportunity to display grace to those who think very badly of us.

Religious illiteracy in society is real, and it leads to bad and ill-informed decisions, as well as causing hurt to those who believe. But in a sense, that's society's problem, not ours.

Instead, I want to challenge those of us who are Christians to concern ourselves with our own lack of cultural and political literacy. To return to our missionary analogy: we do not need to worship the local gods in order to speak the local language. In other words, we can understand our culture and love the people who are comfortable with that culture without having to endorse it or let go of what the Bible teaches.

As Christians, we need to worry more about our own cultural and political literacy if we want to honour God by communicating the gospel in ways that get a hearing. We need to understand our neighbours' beliefs and values if we want to be able to speak to them about why the gospel matters to them today.

We need to understand others and not assume that their aims are malicious. The church's response to LGBT liberation and equality is especially problematic. On one hand, some in the church have indeed begun to follow the local gods at the same time as they have learned the local language, trimming the gospel to suit the culture. There is so much in the Bible that I am uncomfortable about, but I have to humbly accept that I don't have the right to get out the corrector fluid for the bits that I don't like, because God is God and I am not. This should not be controversial. Matthew 5:14 tells us that we are the light of the world, and in the words of Giboney, Wear and Butler in *Compassion (&) Conviction*, this means that

> in order to lead people in the right direction we must base our opinions and actions on what is true, not merely on our preferences or feelings . . . God's ways are not our ways, and we deceive ourselves when we think we know better than God (Isaiah 55:8–9).[11]

Yet this perspective is no longer automatically held by many Christian Millennials, and we must understand why certain parts of the Bible seem intolerant and exclusionary to many Christians today. Perhaps it is largely due to the reactions from others in the church to LGBT people, which have often been clumsy, to put it mildly. The attitude of some has been loveless and bigoted.

In chapter 1, I wrote about a flyer advertising a conference that I was scheduled to speak at. The flyer spoke of the 'gay lobby' in a way that most people would consider disparaging. Was this written by a hateful person? No, I don't think so. But it was written without thought for the culture in which it would be read. I suspect that we can all think of examples. This is why I think that Christians should concern themselves more with becoming culturally and politically literate so that they can respect and relate to their communities. We can affect our own cultural literacy an awful lot more than we can affect the general religious literacy of others. Maybe if we could speak into our culture with more understanding, then people's tendency to misunderstand Christians and Christianity might be alleviated too?

I suspect that the language used by some in the church regarding LGBT issues comes in part from an ignorance of the motives behind

---

11 Justin Giboney, Michael Wear and Chris Butler, *Compassion (&) Conviction: The AND campaign's guide to faithful civic engagement* (Downers Grove, IL: InterVarsity Press, 2020), p. 45.

the drive for LGBT equality. This is ironically and interestingly equivalent to the ignorance within society towards faith issues that underpins the problem of religious illiteracy.

Christians should understand that the conscious motivation of those who propose LGBT equality, and the celebration of LGBT culture and freedoms, is not primarily the erasure of Christian teaching. It really isn't. Instead, the motivation is in seeking an equality that means people are able to live lives of freedom – not being told by the state the type of person with whom they can or cannot form passing or lasting romantic or sexual relationships. It is a reaction to the discrimination against LGBT people that still exists today and has existed in harsher forms in the past.

Although same-sex marriage has been legal in the UK for barely a decade, it is now embedded in the culture. The question we should ask is this: why would anyone oppose it today? A biblical (or other faith-based) understanding of marriage would be one answer. Other non-faith-based standpoints might include objection to marriage per se, but we do need to realize that, in Western societies, such objections or scepticism on this issue now constitute a minority sport.

And if you are a Christian, you are not immune to bigotry on such matters. Sin is our innate opposition to God, our rejection of him and his ways in our lives and in our world. Sin, then, is fundamentally an attitude of heart; it's not an act. Sinful acts are merely the manifestation of that attitude. You can live in opposition to God in a million different ways, and we are not to embrace or celebrate any of those ways, but neither are we to single out specific manifestations and make them out to be 'the great sin'.

If there is no God, if there is no objective natural morality, if there is no eternity, if these few years of life are all we have . . . why does it matter who I have sex with so long as both parties consent? Why does it matter that a foetus isn't permitted to reach full gestation? Why can't I help someone to die if his or her life has become unbearable?

Why should I deny myself, my ambitions, my fulfilment, my financial security and material well-being in order to perform a duty to someone else?

These viewpoints just seem reasonable to people. It then appears that those who oppose such things are the bad guys, because they are the ones seen to be seeking to limit other people's freedoms or judging whether other people's choices are right or wrong.

I confess that I feel the weight of this challenge personally. But I need to remind myself that as a politician I am not here to legislate to make people who aren't Christians live as though they were. As a Christian, I am not here to tell people to stop living this way or that, or to privately simmer with my distaste or disapproval. I have no right to feel such things anyway, because I am a wretched sinner who needs to be forgiven. Some might not think they are sinners, but I know for sure that I am, and I desperately need forgiveness and restoration more than I need air to breathe.

As a Christian, if I love people as I am commanded to do, then surely I want people to see Jesus. I want them to hear the gospel of grace and forgiveness and eternal life, and I want them to respond.

If we want to speak the gospel into this society, we need to take the time to understand it.

Put more bluntly: do we realize how we are heard? Do we want to make it easier or harder for the opponents of the gospel to characterize us as they want to?

Hillary Clinton spoke of those supporting Donald Trump in the 2016 US presidential election as 'a basket of deplorables'. She may have meant to refer to the white-supremacist Ku Klux Klan members who had declared their support for Trump, but the reality is that millions of working-class, non-metropolitan people with fairly traditional values heard her say this and assumed that she meant them too. More generally, in recent times the liberal left (of which I am a member) has had a habit of sneering at or demonizing those who don't wholly buy into their world view. But this is increasingly a practice of those who hold strong feelings on both sides of a debate. The whole notion of 'cancel culture' has arisen because people increasingly find it hard to separate the views of their opponents from their worth as human beings. Particularly on social media, arguments can quickly escalate beyond the issue being discussed to abuse and threats based on someone's character, looks, family and sometimes their very right to life. We must be so careful not to fall into this way of thinking and behaving.

The lesson that Christians, liberals and also those on the right of the political spectrum need to learn is that if you want the people to listen to your message, you must not behave as if you don't like them! Don't wrinkle your noses, disapproving of their lifestyles and all that they hold to be important! I mean, who do we think we are? Christians believe that we are all sinners, and that Christ died for us before we had come to trust in him, indeed while we were still his enemies. So those people you disapprove of, the society that cleaves to behaviours and values that are unchristian . . . Jesus died for them! Have a word with yourself!

Jesus came to heal the sick, not the healthy. He didn't pretend they weren't sick, but neither did he deal with their issues by mocking them or finding them distasteful. A key difference between Christians and non-Christians is not that Christians are any less sick than non-Christians, but that we have realized we need a doctor.

In his ministry on earth, Jesus spent a great deal of time interacting with religious leaders – respectable and senior people who were the insiders in his society. The New Testament documents, though, suggest that he spent yet more time – and much more of his 'leisure' time – with people who were considered outsiders. Tax collectors (a byword for dishonesty and collaboration with the imperialist occupier), prostitutes, sexual sinners of other kinds, people who weren't religiously observant, racial outcasts, people with disabilities, or physical conditions such as leprosy, or behavioural aberrations that made them social pariahs . . .

Many of these people knew their need of Jesus. Some were outcasts by dint of their life choices, others because of the rotten hand they had been dealt. All of them would have been sneered at or at least avoided by the self-righteous, respectable insiders.

The last thing a Christian should ever want to be is a self-righteous, respectable insider.

Yet, sadly, we sometimes see that Christians share an ugly characteristic with the so-called 'liberal elite': we know we are right, and we look down at and condemn those who don't get it.

I don't think that is a humble or godly attitude, and I am certain that it is a counterproductive one.

People aren't facing being lost for eternity without God because of who they sleep with, what they spend their money on, the fact that they had an abortion or that they do not care for their parents in old age. These are just symptoms of a deeper problem. They're lost because they are sinners who have not accepted the free gift of salvation by grace through faith in Jesus Christ. So let's tell them about him, which means being in awe of God and faithful to his teaching, and full of love and gentleness towards those we want to see saved, seeking to understand them and to speak their language, as we open their eyes to the reality of the one who loves them more than they could ever hope or imagine.

Case study: Michael Wear

As a young, politicized student, Michael Wear got the date of a conference wrong, and as he walked out of the hotel, embarrassed and dejected, he saw a young hotshot senator by the name of Barack Obama walking in. Michael approached him, there being no Secret Service security detail, and told him he wanted to work for him.

The senator announced a presidential run a few days later, and within ten months Michael was with Obama in Iowa, then in

Chicago, then in the White House, working at the very top as a religious adviser.

Michael grew up in a blue-collar Catholic family in America's Rust Belt. He was political from a young age. His grandfather was a 'labor union' man (trade union in the UK) and, while not explicitly political, was always civically minded. When Michael became a Christian at fifteen, he initially considered becoming a pastor, before someone took him aside and advised him that there are in fact plenty of Christians who are not pastors! Instead, following his interest and increasing passion for theology and for politics led to the central vocational question of his life: 'What does it mean to be faithful in public things?'

Michael is an unusual political creature – a white evangelical Christian who is also a Democrat. He points out that this is partly because his family were typical blue-collar Democrats. But also, he felt the conviction of Scripture as he grew in theological and political understanding, leading him to want to work against societal injustice and poverty. But, Michael is quick to point out, the issue of how Christians align their faith with politics is one where our cultural illiteracy becomes clear.

'The Christian faith has incredible resources for our social and political lives, not just our personal lives. But as C. S. Lewis wrote, Christianity does not offer a particular political pro-gramme, and when we reduce it to that ... we do a great disservice to the gospel.' In the USA particularly, there is a great conflation of faith with a political party, as if the Republican Party were the only party acceptable to Christians. Not only is this an unhelpful attitude, it is simply wrong – 'two thirds of the Democrat Party are people of faith'. Michael has prayed with Obama in the White House, and can bear witness to Joe Biden's personal faith.

That is not to deny, of course, that there is a major religious literacy problem with Democratic elites. Indeed, the problem exists among 'elites in American life in general, which won't be unfamiliar in the UK but is new in the US ... There's an impression among some that there are great levels of antagonism among Democrats for people of faith. In my experience there are very few people who wake up in the morning thinking: *How do I go after religious freedom today?*'

Michael sees the decline in cultural Christianity not as something to be mourned but as a historical moment we should seize. 'There are pockets of indifference and a lack of familiarity which is a great gospel opportunity ... we have the honour of sharing the gospel with people in our own neighbourhoods who have never heard it before ... You've got people who did not grow up in Christian homes; people who went to schools where Christianity was not part of the environment. What an incredible opportunity!'

We should not spend our time fretting about the religious illiteracy of the surrounding culture. Instead, we should make sure we are not culturally illiterate. Then the gospel can be shared in a way that speaks to people's lives and place and time. Paul preached the same gospel but in different ways, whether discussing the Scriptures in synagogues (Acts 17:2) or quoting poets in Greek temples (Acts 17:22–31). In the same way, we should seek to learn how our culture thinks so that we can fully engage with it, sharing the gospel and living as faithful witnesses.

Part 2

WHY CHRISTIANS SHOULD ENGAGE WITH POLITICS

4

Because the Bible is bigger than politics

It was a hot day in June 2015. The Liberal Democrat leadership campaign was heating up too. In a glass-walled room in the Gloucestershire County Cricket Club in Bristol, my fellow leadership contender Norman Lamb and I were being grilled in more ways than one.

There are quite a lot of Liberal Democrats in the south-west of England, so the room (that glass-walled room) was absolutely crammed full.

Did I mention that it was hot? It was really hot!

Maybe that gives me an excuse for losing my temper.

At one point a party member in the audience asked me, rather aggressively, 'Which comes first for you: God or the Liberal Democrats?'

I didn't completely blow my top, but my answer was forceful, angry and blunt. 'You'd only ask that question if you didn't know where this party came from!' I then launched into a lecture about the Liberal Party's nineteenth-century origins as a movement that argued for religious liberty and, in particular, for the right of Nonconformist 'evangelical' Christians to have equality with those who belonged to the established church. I then snapped that if we had become a party that had no room for people of faith, then we were absolutely not a liberal party any more.

It was an effective response. It went down well (apart from with the bloke who asked the question). Maybe if I'd carried on like this, and been more combative in my answers to questions about my

43

Christianity, rather than looking like a terminally angst-ridden rabbit in the headlights, I might have done a better job?

Who knows . . . but the eagle-eyed among you will have noticed that I didn't actually give a direct answer to that question. So, which comes first for you, Tim? God or the Liberal Democrats? Short answer: God, of course. Better and longer answer: these are incomparable entities. You cannot equate God to a political movement, or faith in the God of the Bible to an ideology.

Members of faith communities are often subject to discrimination because society assumes that we have divided loyalties; we will be asked whether our first allegiance is to the UK, or to Rome, Israel, the Bible, the Qur'an. There is a suspicion among some that we're at least a little treacherous. The same applies *within* political parties: people think that if you believe in God, then your loyalty must be mixed.

Actually, yes, that's true.

There are many passages in the Bible that tell us that as Christians we are aliens or strangers in the world (Philippians 3:20; Hebrews 11:13–16; 1 Peter 2:11). In the context of the Roman world of the New Testament, this would have been understood to mean that we are foreigners in a province set up by the empire as an outpost, for example Philippi, Thessalonica or Corinth, where the emperor's proxy would administer justice and he would perhaps visit.[1] We are citizens of the kingdom of heaven, but we live in the province of earth. But we must always bear in mind that God promises one day not to abolish the earth but to join it with heaven, and to redeem and rule over all.

The phrase 'foreigners and exiles' in 1 Peter 2:11 is sometimes translated as 'sojourners', and the US Christian organization that has taken this name describes its people as being 'fully present in the world but committed to a different order'.[2] This is an excellent

---

1   Tom Wright explains this well in *Surprised by Hope* (London: SPCK, 2007), ch. 8.
2   <https://sojo.net/about/about-sojourners> (accessed 3 July 2022).

description of our time on earth. We are supposed to rub up against our culture but also to be present in it.

Christianity is countercultural and will at times seem (at best) peculiar in any non-Christian context. If your parents, friends, spouse or children aren't Christians, then much of your outlook and behaviour as a Christian will go against the grain and seem odd or even offensive.

This will also go for any political party you may belong to. The Bible says some jarring things about loving God more than you love your nearest and dearest. Matthew in his Gospel account records Jesus commending those who would forsake brothers, sisters, fathers or mothers for the sake of Christ. That's a hard thing for us to hear – but we know that God is not anti-family and we know he is not cruel, which must mean that Jesus is not saying we shouldn't love deeply those close to us. He must be making a different kind of point, then. It's this: we love our families more and we love them better, more selflessly and more completely if we love them in response to Jesus' breathtaking love for us and with the selfless love that he pours into our hearts.

Now, I don't want to feed your suspicion that the Liberal Democrats are basically a cult, but I often talk about my party as a family. I absolutely stand by that. As I seek to put Jesus first in my life and – in response to his grace towards me – serve and obey him in love, I find that my love for the people in my Lib Dem family grows, and my desire to serve them and my local community also grows. It's a better love and a better loyalty than if I didn't make Jesus more important than the Lib Dems. This might sound odd, but because I seek to follow Jesus it means that my love for my party is less selfish, less bound up with pride, more giving, more forgiving.

So, to that bloke in that hot room at the cricket club the answer is this: 'God comes first, but the Liberal Democrats are better off as a result . . . and I'm sorry I lost my rag.'

In any event, being a Christian and being a member of a political party are very different things. The Bible is not a manifesto.

I joined the Liberal Party at sixteen because I agreed with many of its policies and because I bought into the values of individual liberty, internationalism and care for our environment. I was also attracted to the culture and ethos of the party: working hard for local communities. In an age of ideological extremes, I was drawn to the Liberals because despite their strong ideals there was a humility about their cause, a belief that 'no-one has a monopoly on good ideas'. Liberalism felt reasonable; it didn't proclaim that it had sole ownership of the truth.

Yet I became a Christian at eighteen, having become convinced by its claim to ultimate truth. Before then, I knew very few Christians, but I had a sense that Christianity was OK so long as you didn't take it too seriously. I felt that Jesus probably had existed but it was just a fairy tale to think of him as divine; Jesus was a good teacher, that's all. Furthermore, I thought that the church was an instrument used to control us and make us conform . . . and 'born-again Christians' were just weird and held intolerant, illiberal views. To be fair, the one born-again Christian I really knew – Jack – was a lovely, funny, interesting guy. But Christians I knew from afar seemed strange and dull, and their lives looked very unattractive. They took things too seriously, they couldn't have fun, they believed ludicrous things. In short, Christianity appeared irrelevant, intolerant, unattractive, untrue. It is safe to say that I was not particularly drawn to this movement.

My moment of 'conversion' came reluctantly.

In the early hours of the morning, sitting beneath a whirring fan in my room in Singapore, having read the Bible and books on prophecy and apologetics for what felt like days on end, it struck me, with an almost physical force: *Flipping heck, it's true!*

Unlike my opinion of Liberal Party policy, I didn't agree with much of what I read in the Bible. It disturbed me, it contradicted what I thought, it wasn't what I wanted to be true. But the evidence for Jesus' existence, death and resurrection, for the truth of his staggering claims, won me over. As did his amazing love for me.

To become a Christian is to give your life to Jesus, to hand it over, to resign command. Becoming a Christian is ego-shattering. It involves humility, but actually, it is not crushing. It's the opposite, because you are handing control over to one who will never let you down, who is perfect and who loves you so completely that he can and will only ever act in your interests.

This tremendous sense that 'it's all true' stripped away my considerable defences and my deep objection to the very idea of becoming a Christian, to becoming someone like those weirdos I knew . . . But those objections were very strong; in fact, I recall that I really didn't want Christianity to be true.

First of all, it felt frightening – that there is a 'meta-reality' to the universe, a supreme being, a judgment that I will face, a sovereign hand over everything, a God who is so awesome he just spoke this unimaginably vast and complex universe into existence and yet is so personal and tender that he understands and knows intimately everything about me . . . and cares about it all, indeed cares about me. Oh yes, this is wonderful, but it is also terrifying. I found it terrifying in itself, and I also feared what people would think of me for having come to believe that this was true.

The second reason I didn't want Christianity to be true was that I knew it meant I had to hand my life over to Christ. It meant doing stuff I didn't feel like doing, and not doing stuff I really did feel like doing. Above all else, I sensed that if I became a Christian then I was surrendering control; I could no longer pretend that I was in charge of me. Eighteen-year-old men have a habit of assuming that they are the centre of the universe, but I now knew that I wasn't even the centre of myself.

But if Christianity is true, if God is real, if the Bible can be trusted, if Jesus is exactly who he claimed to be . . . then my objections must be discarded. As I came to understand much later, if there is a real God then the last thing you will expect him to do is to endorse your existing values, opinions and lifestyle. If he is perfect and you are not, then you would expect the real God to disturb you, contradict you, turn much of what you took for granted on its head. If your God doesn't shatter your world view in this way, you have surely invented him.

So, none of this is comparable to choosing to join a political party. I thought Paddy Ashdown was great; some may even say that I idolized him. I certainly made vast sacrifices in his service. But ideologies, political parties and politicians make very disappointing gods. Ideologies can help us make sense of the world and give us an approach through which we can organize society and the economy and even make the world better. Parties are vehicles for bringing those ideas and approaches into practice, and politicians can inspire and lead people towards those goals.

Surely, we have all lived long enough to know that if we look to politics to deliver ultimate satisfaction and hope, we can only end up crushed. It doesn't mean that politics isn't a noble and utterly worthwhile endeavour; I know from personal experience that it is.

I joined the Liberals first; then two years later I became a Christian. If this was a neat testimony, I would have done it the other way round. But this isn't a neat testimony – it's a real one with all the imperfections we should expect. It would be far more convenient for my purposes in this book to say that having become a Christian, with my heart in tune with God's desire for justice and mercy and with a Spirit-driven desire to serve my community, I chose to involve myself in politics. It didn't happen that way for me.

As a young person, affected by the society around me, touched by injustices that I saw, persuaded by ideas and policies and drawn to individuals who impressed me and with whom I felt a strong affinity, I signed on the dotted line and became a Liberal. I got my membership card; I found out when the first meeting was; I threw myself into this new world which began to consume much of my social life, my free time and my meagre finances. I loved it, I felt a sense of purpose and belonging, and I stopped being bored with everything – an amazing state for a sixteen-year-old lad to find himself in!

Now, in the account above, there are of course some superficial similarities with a conversion to Christianity. I don't think we need to get too hung up on that, but certainly when I became a Christian the epic and eternal nature of that truth meant I now had come face to face with what I believed to be ultimate reality. My politics had to either fit in with that ultimate reality or else be discarded. As I said, there is nothing neat about my story. Jesus Christ came to save flaky, imperfect sinners like me. He didn't come to save super-sorted people who have their lives in order, because those people don't really exist. So in practice, I fudged. As a young man I lived a kind of double existence: reading more of the Bible, spending time with other Christians and praying – and then going to Lib Dem meetings, organizing, campaigning and enjoying the social life that went with it.

That throwaway remark from my friend – that perhaps politics was too much of a mucky business for a Christian to be involved in – was powerful. I shrugged it off at the time, but it's often come back to me since. In fact, being involved in politics in the way I chose to be involved did keep me from a deeper commitment to Jesus. Too many parties, too much drink, young attractive women . . . mostly alongside people who weren't Christians and who weren't therefore going to help me to be accountable.

But as I have pondered and prayed over that challenge, over whether politics is just a mucky business that I should avoid, I have come to consider the vocation of politics to be one that gives me the chance to do good, to serve people and to bring opportunities to point people to Jesus. In my role as an MP I think of the families I've been able to reunite by taking on the immigration system, the hundreds of people facing homelessness whom we've been able to house, those experiencing health emergencies I have been able to secure care for . . . all because I won some elections and got the right to hold an office I have made use of so that I can fight the corner of people who had nowhere else to turn. I've also found myself with a profile that allows me to share the gospel publicly. I couldn't have done that if I'd washed my hands of that mucky business.

When I became an MP in 2005, I asked myself what was expected of me, not just as an MP but as a Christian MP. I noted that some Christian MPs focused on campaigning and legislating to put biblical morality into practice in UK society – specifically on those matters to do with sexual behaviour and identity, which we might consider to be self-regarding matters of personal morality. I respected those MPs, but it felt to me then, as it does now, that this isn't what we are called to do. If everyone is created equally in the image of God, and if everyone is also a sinner, then we must be sure not to give the impression that God thinks less of some sinners than others. Also, it feels counterproductive for Christians to seek to legislate to make people who are not Christians live as though they were. I cannot see the point in this, and to me it feels coercive and wrong – illiberal even. Edmund Burke once said that all the laws against non-believers 'have not saved one single soul'.[3] So that's how a person whose theology isn't at all 'liberal' can at the same time be a political liberal. Of course there are tensions, but there are tensions of different sorts for Christians in *all* political parties.

I joined the Liberal Party at sixteen. I became a Christian at eighteen. These are major moments in my life, but they are not equivalent events.

Moved by injustices I saw in the world around me, convinced that the Liberal Party was a vehicle for me to do something about those injustices and agreeing with most of the party's policies, I shelled out £1.50 and joined up.

---

3 In fact the quote, in a time when Catholics were discriminated against, was: 'all the laws against the popery have not saved one single soul'. Source: 'Tracts Relative to the Laws against Popery in Ireland' (1760–1765).

Becoming a Christian two years later was different. I didn't read the Sermon on the Mount and think: *I agree with that! Where do I sign up? When's the first meeting? When will my membership card arrive in the post?*

As a Christian I see politics as a way of serving people, of serving God in the public square. Society needs leadership, governments have to exist, and politicians all follow some kind of ideology or belief framework in order to come to decisions.

There are countless imperfect frameworks that allow imperfect people to organize imperfect societies and ensure that they are imperfectly governed. The Liberal Democrats are my chosen vehicle of imperfection. But we need Christians in the other political parties too. One of the many reasons I choose the Liberal Democrats is that true liberalism understands that it is not right to impose belief systems on others. Liberalism also possesses a wisdom that I believe to be absent in authoritarianism and libertarianism: an understanding that freedom is vital to human dignity but that freedoms often compete and so we have to make choices to limit some liberties in order to enhance and protect those which are more important . . . but that's for an entirely different book!

Christianity, however, tells us that there is ultimate truth and that while we have important needs here on earth – food, work, health, education, a home, safety, a clean environment – we also have a much greater need. When Jesus meets the Samaritan woman, the account of which is recorded in John chapter 4, we see a conversation about the most basic apparent human need – water – turn into one about our biggest actual need: a relationship with Jesus, forged by his death in our place to secure our total forgiveness and reunification with the God who yearns for relationship with us.

Being in a political party gives me the ability to join forces with friends who share opinions and objectives so that we can campaign together to make things better for the people we share this planet with.

Being a Christian gives me ultimate meaning and an eternal, redeeming relationship with the God of the universe. As I live in that relationship with God, my politics gives me a chance to live a life in this world where I can do good, and while my politics must never be my god, I am nevertheless motivated all the more, and with greater sincerity and compassion, to serve in my political work because I am seeking to follow Jesus as my Lord.

Case study: Sir Steve Webb

In 2010, Liberal Democrat MP Steve Webb found himself in an exceptional position for a member of a third party: he was asked to be a minister in a coalition government. It wasn't a difficult decision – he cared about the issues covered by the Department of Work and Pensions (known as the DWP). The catch? He would have to work alongside Conservative Party colleagues, and would answer directly to the new Secretary of State – former Conservative Party leader Iain Duncan Smith.

There was initially some wariness between the two men when the coalition began. As Steve says: 'his politics and mine couldn't be further apart', one a Brexiteer, the other a Remainer. But Steve went in also with a respect for the motivations behind Duncan Smith's work. When Duncan Smith stepped down as party leader, whereas many would have left Parliament to earn lots of money in the City, he stayed put and set up the Centre for Social Justice instead. Ultimately, Webb and Duncan Smith recognized that their shared Christian faith provided a foundation for a shared motivation to bring about the common good.

This 'mutual respect and mutual loyalty' in a coalition government marked by suspicion between the parties was a rare glimpse of a better way. The two politicians eventually built a trusting relationship and a 'strong bond' across party lines. Each learned that they could trust the other and that confidences would be respected. Several other Christians were also working in the department, including a special adviser and a Permanent Secretary – so much so that the DWP became known as the 'Department for Worship and Prayer'!

This is not to say that Steve's political convictions became mushy and tainted. In fact, over the coalition years there were profound political disagreements. For instance, when the Treasury attempted to enact a policy to put undue financial pressure on welfare claimants to go back to work, his was a leading voice in pushing back against it.

Since losing his seat in 2015 Steve has remained friends with a group of former colleagues who would meet regularly to pray as a group – two Labour, two Conservative, one Unionist and himself as a Lib Dem. Those bonds of friendship and fellowship 'go deeper than the tribes that separate us'. It was typical to 'have a meal together and go off to vote – three of us would vote one way, three the other, and we would come back for pudding'.

This tension between fellowship and strong political conviction was a constant. Their friendship didn't mean that their political beliefs were not sincere, but it recognized that 'there are things more important than that'. Politics and policy matter deeply. But they are fleeting, and 'Jesus Christ is the same yesterday, today and for ever' (Hebrews 13:8).

5

Because we are more radical than we think

I don't like being called a conservative. My politics aren't conservative, my music taste isn't conservative, my dress sense isn't . . . well, OK, I dress like a dad. I wear politically incorrect *Father Ted* T-shirts when I think no-one is looking and – in my head – I think I'm proper edgy. (Who am I kidding?) But my theology – *that's* conservative, isn't it? Am I not a 'conservative evangelical'?

Forgive me, but I hate that label. Not just because I've got a prejudice against the word 'conservative' due to its party political connotations, but also because I just don't think it's an accurate description of a Christian who believes that 'all Scripture is God-breathed' (2 Timothy 3:16) and seeks to be guided by the Holy Spirit.

I think this for two reasons. First, I call myself an *orthodox* Christian because, although I accept that some people draw different conclusions from their reading of the Bible, I don't feel the need to add to it through concern that we can somehow improve God's Word. Neither am I one who subtracts things from the Bible because some bits make me feel uncomfortable and so out comes the corrector fluid.[1]

---

1 Of course, the Bible is not simply a list of rules or doctrines, and Christians over the centuries have spilled much ink, breath and blood in arguing from the Bible for different ideas of God's will. Ultimately, it is the greatest story we will ever hear; one that teaches us about God and about ourselves. It is made up of different genres of literature – poetry, letters, narrative, parables, books of the law, prophecy, wisdom literature, etc. All of these are read in translation from the original Hebrew or Greek, and we need to recognize them within their own historical contexts – what they intended to convey to their original hearers – but also to seek the guidance of the Holy Spirit in revealing eternal truths that are current for us today. We also need to be aware that we all read the Bible through the lens of our own culture, church tradition, the books we have read and the preaching we have heard. We need to weigh it all carefully. This is why we talk about *studying* the Bible, both collectively and individually: it is a lifelong journey. To explore this further, we would recommend getting hold of a good

I don't doubt that those who fit those descriptors are thoughtful and sincere in their faith, but it seems to me that some of these views do not have a sufficiently ambitious view of God, who he is and what he is capable of.

Me? I accept the Bible as the expression of God's authority, telling the great story of God's love for us and his redeeming grace offered to us through Jesus and revealed to us through the Holy Spirit.[2] I seek to read it prayerfully and with a heart open to his guidance. I argue that this makes me an orthodox Christian, in the 'centre ground'.

But my second reason for objecting to being called 'conservative' is that Christianity just *isn't* conservative – it is utterly, mind-blowingly radical! Seriously, it makes communism or anarchism look as square and dull as an episode of *Terry and June* (kids, you'll just have to look that up online).

Christianity is radical in so many ways, but let me pick just a few.

If you live in the West today, you live in the most individualistic culture – largely as a result of the political philosophy of liberalism – the world has ever seen. The law and the social norms of this age give you unprecedented freedom to choose (well, they did until the virus came along). Of course, in practice your choices are often limited by your circumstances, educational opportunities, family background and financial situation, but in theory you can choose where you live, your line of work, to be your own boss in the 'workplace', who you'll marry, what gender you will identify as, whether and how to reproduce, when and where you will find your entertainment, your virtual identity, and so much more and in so much more variety than has ever been available to us before. On top of this, you live at a time when you can broadcast this identity that you have shaped to a watching world.

---

book on *how* to read the Bible, such as *How to Read the Bible for All Its Worth* by Gordon D. Fee and Douglas Stuart (Bletchley: Scripture Union, 1993).

2   N. T. Wright, *Scripture and the Authority of God* (London: SPCK, 2005), is helpful in unpacking what Christians mean when we refer to the Bible as having authority as the 'Word of God'.

Andy Warhol famously predicted that 'in the future, everyone will be famous for fifteen minutes'. In 1968, that sounded a bit of a stretch of the imagination. Today, it is a colossal understatement. Now, everyone is famous all the time. At least, everyone who goes on social media. People live out their perfect lives, sharing pictures of their perfect children, their perfect opinions and their perfect soufflés on their social media feeds to an audience that may not be in the millions but nevertheless is an audience.

Never has the emphasis on 'me being me' and 'you being you' been so huge.

Christianity, being countercultural, contradicts this pervasive world view, saying: 'Actually, you don't belong to you – you have a far higher purpose.' There is nothing more radical and disturbing than that.

Psalm 24:1 tells us: 'The earth is the LORD's, and everything in it'. Following our departure from the EU, there continues to be a debate in the UK about sovereignty, and the Bible has something to say about ultimate sovereignty. There is a sovereign – and it isn't me or you; we aren't even sovereign over our own bodies. Yet, the fact that you belong to God isn't some haughty declaration; it is wrapped in real tenderness and intimacy. Nowhere does this seem more evident than in Psalm 139: 'you knit me together in my mother's womb . . . I am fearfully and wonderfully made . . .' God literally knows you inside out. The hairs on your head are numbered. He knows every cell of your body because he put them in place and made them into you.

For those of us who put their trust in Jesus Christ, the claim is even more personal. Isaiah 43:1 (ESV) moves me deeply: 'I have called you by name, you are mine.' What an antidote this is to our culture's radical individualism!

The individualism that dominates our Western culture offers us liberation from religion, rules, doctrines and demands. Liberalism makes it possible to have the freedom to believe different things, including the freedom to reject God altogether. Yet ironically, when taken to its extreme expression, this freedom leads us to kill off God, and replaces him with a different god – and that god is you. So in the end, you aren't liberated at all. You are now a slave to a god who isn't all that powerful, isn't all that good and isn't all that wise. You may be a very nice person, but you are a rubbish god. You can only disappoint you.

There isn't radicalism in this world view at all, just adherence to a new religion. 'Religious' people believe they must do 'good' or perform in a certain way in order to put a god in their debt or to earn society's approval or acceptance. However, Christians realize they are in God's debt and that this debt was paid on the cross, and so they live, radically liberated, from the need to tick boxes and obey laws in order to win approval. Instead, they can enter a freed state of wanting to follow Christ and to live for him because they are overwhelmed by his love and purpose for them. Nothing in Karl Marx's *Das Kapital* gets even close to this; it is utterly revolutionary.

Paul in 1 Corinthians 6:19–20 puts it like this: 'You are not your own; you were bought at a price.'

You were bought. From whom, or from what? You were bought and freed from slavery to your own shifting and inadequate standards, to feeding your desires and living with your back turned to the one who made you and loves you. And the price was the infinite agony experienced by Jesus Christ on your behalf.

The writer of the letter to the Hebrews gives us a precious insight into the mind of Jesus: 'For the joy that was set before him he endured the cross, scorning its shame' (Hebrews 12:2). I believe this passage tells us that although the agony and shame of the cross was horrific beyond anyone's imagination, Jesus considered it all to be worth it because there was a greater joy on the other side. That joy was saving and knowing you. If that doesn't move you to tears, then keep rereading it and meditating on it until it does, because it will.

Grace is the unmerited favour of God towards human beings, seen most powerfully but not exclusively at the cross.

Grace is deeply radical – and hugely disruptive to the current dominant world view. In response to God's grace, we are led to reflect that grace in our dealings with everyone else. That's not how the world behaves! We are nice to people we like or approve of, but never to those we find distasteful, or those we strongly disagree with. We must condemn or 'cancel' them. The world tells us that when people wrong us or make a statement that doesn't chime with our values, we are to shame them and shun them – not love them and forgive them!

The parable of the good Samaritan in Luke 10 is shocking stuff. Jesus has been asked: 'Who is my neighbour?', and he tells the famous parable which gives the answer: everyone is your neighbour, including your enemy, and you are to love your neighbour, and that love should cost you, because all genuine love does. So let's be clear, then: that person on social media who voted the other way in the EU referendum and posts stuff you really hate – you are to love that person and make sacrifices for him or her.

You may be able to think of even worse people than that person who voted the 'wrong' way . . . and yes, you're meant to love them too!

This is scandalous stuff.

God is the source of all justice, so if the person in question has committed a crime then he or she is to be punished appropriately, but our attitude to those who offend us is to be loving. We will of course fail to do this sometimes, and that's where God's grace comes in because his death pays for that failure as it does for every other.

Are you outraged by this? Good, because it *is* outrageous. Tim Keller's excellent book on the parable of the prodigal son is titled *The Prodigal God*, which some might think is a bit disrespectful, but the word 'prodigal' implies a lavish extravagance, a recklessness with our resources. That is exactly what God does: he gives everything because he wants you, he loves you. Let's not be like the unfaithful servant in Matthew 18, forgiven a vast debt by the king yet unwilling to forgive a smaller debt owed to him by his co-worker.

Look at US politics over the last few years, or the UK during and since Brexit, the sabre-rattling by political and cultural foes on social media, the debates that now descend into more than just ideological disagreement but have evolved into despising the other view and the other person as morally repugnant . . . How explosive and shocking would it be if grace broke out?

What a challenge to the established approach of all ideologies, where the wrong stay wrong and the enemy remains the enemy! Not so for the uniquely radical world view of Christianity, which tells us that Jesus died for us while we were still God's enemies (Romans 5:10).

So we aren't to grasp for what is rightfully ours, to demand revenge, to settle old scores. We aren't to despise, or to covet or fear; instead, we are to stand in God's amazing grace and seek to reflect that in all our attitudes and actions.

Christianity is astonishingly radical in what it says on personal sovereignty and grace, but in every area the Bible challenges and contradicts established norms in ways that, in comparison, make the gulf between Lenin and Nicholas II look so surmountable that all it would take is a Clegg–Cameron-style Rose Garden press conference . . .

On justice – where else will you find a view that doesn't just say that justice *should* or *must* be done, but confidently tells us that justice *will* be done? A view that says no evil deed will ever go unpunished – not one? I visited Auschwitz in 2009 with some sixth-formers from my constituency. It was a cold February day, and as we filed, shivering, past the forlorn belongings, including the shorn hair, of a fraction of those millions murdered in the gas chambers, I felt a deep anger and then shuddered at a thought that entered my head without warning, a thought that was at the same time frightening and satisfying: *Thank God there's a hell.* I was shocked by my own internal monologue – and yet I stand by it. Thank God there is justice. Thank God that not one of those atrocities is forgotten, not one of those victims is out of the Lord's mind. Justice is more than an ideal to Christians; it is a confident expectation, and it should drive how we treat one another today – because if we demand justice, and we should, we must also remember that we too deserve judgment for our wrong deeds and attitudes. How can God be good and merciful, and at the same time be just and righteous? The cross gives us our answer as justice is meted out on all wickedness, while mercy dictates that it is the sinless one, God himself, who takes that judgment upon himself.

And then there is love. Love is everywhere. We are told to love ourselves, to love whomever we choose, to love love itself . . . and yet this twenty-first-century Western brand of love isn't worthy of the name. Love in the Bible is real and radical, and it is nearly always self-sacrificial. It is truly eternal, and the love we receive from God – if we are prepared to receive it – quenches every thirst and satisfies the deep and indescribable yearning within us. The love that God has for us is personal; it is eternal, it is unshakeable, it is passionate and it is costly to him. Indeed, love in the Bible is always practical. It is shown through sacrifice and giving, because true love costs – it isn't selfish. Seen at its purest, it is present at the cross of Calvary where God himself redeemed us by shedding his own blood.

Romantic love and sexual love are good. The Song of Songs in the Old Testament is a wonderful celebration of a sensual relationship – an entire book of the Bible devoted to one of the great threads running through creation. Yet romantic love now seems utterly central to our cultural narrative of what constitutes human flourishing. Following our hearts, finding true love, finding true happiness . . . these things are so much more of a big deal in our culture today than they once were. Why? Because there is nothing else. There is no eternity, there is no ultimate justice or purpose, there is nothing else to live for; so maybe, just maybe, I can get twenty or thirty years of idealized (but probably not realized) happiness with my partner before age or cancer or a traffic accident whisks one of us away?

I'm a barrel of laughs, I know . . . but I want to be honest with you. Christianity radically holds a mirror up to the reality of our culture, and it pulls no punches. The gospel is such good news, but you really won't grasp how good the good news is until you have understood how bad the bad news is.

When it comes to understanding the nature of existence, I suggest that there really are only two credible world views. Both are radical, and yet everything else is simply intellectually lazy. The first tells us that there is an all-powerful God who is the source of all meaning and morality and the deliverer of all justice; the second asserts that there is no God and that there is no meaning, no morality and no justice.

If you don't believe in God, if all 'creation' is a mindless and temporary accident, then everything you achieve or desire, everything you are, every feeling you have, every relationship, every triumph and every disaster, everything that you take pride in . . . is of no lasting consequence. You are a collection of atoms; you will last a few decades, then you will die, your consciousness gone for ever, never again to be stirred; the planet on which you briefly lived will die, burned up by our sun as it becomes a swollen red giant before fizzling out altogether, and then as the ages pass, one by one all the lights in the sky will go out until there is nothing. Lifeless, pointless, nothing. So, when people do evil, we can't really say that they are evil because who is to say what is good or evil? These are just arbitrary human terms that have no meaning. There is no basis for condemning lies, physical abuse, theft, cruelty or infidelity because there are no virtues to transgress, nor is there any lasting meaning in anything.

Now, I want to be clear that I don't believe any of that, but unless you are determined to lie to yourself, it's all you've got left if you've killed off God. Friedrich Nietzsche used the phrase 'God is dead' in 1882, but despite his own atheism, this was no triumphant declaration – it was an acknowledgment of a crisis:

> When one gives up the Christian faith, one pulls the right to Christian morality out from under one's feet. This morality is by no means self-evident. By breaking one main concept out of Christianity, the faith in God, one breaks the whole: nothing necessary remains in one's hands.[3]

And so we make up our own rules, our own norms, our own morality. As we seek desperately to de-Christianize our Western society, the values that were grounded in the gospel – justice, grace, acceptance of God's creative sovereignty, the right to life, the humility that comes with knowing you are not your own – they all start to fade out. We build our own hell.

The slightly better news, of course, is that atheists are also made in the image of God and have his moral laws imprinted in their heart. Sorry to break it to you, guys, but you didn't actually kill God at all . . .

I know this is disturbing stuff, but it goes to the heart of why Christianity is the countercultural, utterly disturbing, radically transformative world view that knocks every other philosophy and ideology into a cocked hat.

Christianity isn't just countercultural to *this* culture; it's *always* countercultural. Jesus healed and did good on the sabbath, rather than doing the nothing that was expected of him by the social and religious norms of that time. Christians in the second- and third-century Roman Empire cared for the sick abandoned by everyone else during deadly plagues – probably smallpox – because love, to them, was practical and self-sacrificial, and eternity was a reality.

---

3 Friedrich Nietzsche, *Twilight of the Idols* (1889).

Many Christians opposed slavery in the eighteenth and nineteenth centuries because every person is made in the image of God and carries ultimate and equal dignity. For the same reasons, many Christians opposed the despicable standards in the factories of the newly industrialized West, and today it is Christians who maintain that the God who made us and loves us knows far better what is good for our flourishing than we do. In every age, Christianity is mocked and called outdated by those who hold certain world views – views that have mostly since become extinct themselves. Meanwhile, Christianity survives and grows, forever relevant, forever real, forever radical.

This is why we should care about politics and get involved in politics, not just by bringing this radical message to our confused society but also by working it out practically in our committed engagement with that society.

Case study: Peter Hitchens

Peter Hitchens has had a career in journalism that is striking for the fervour of his views and the colourful force of his language. He has reported from places as diverse as communist Moscow, the campaign trail in Thatcher's Britain, and the White House in the Clinton administration. His politics has shifted with time – 'and age' – from radical socialism to social conservatism. As writer Anthony Howard said of him in one book review: 'the old revolutionary socialist has lost nothing of his passion and indignation ... It is merely the convictions that have changed, not the fervour and fanaticism with which they continue to be held.'[4]

Initially, Peter found atheism at school an 'extremely appealing creed'. It promised 'liberty from constraint', and he told everyone

4 Anthony Howard, '*The Broken Compass: How British Politics Lost Its Way* by Peter Hitchens', review, *New Statesman*, 21 May 2009.

who cared to listen. He burned his Bible on Cambridge playing fields. He was an 'actively hostile, scoffing atheist'. He came back to his Christian faith in his thirties when looking at a medieval doom painting. The pivotal moment came when he gazed at the painting and considered: *Maybe there is justice in the universe. And if so, which side will I be on?*

As an Anglican, Peter is quick to defend the role of faith in the state. The established Church of England's parish system over 'every square inch of the country does have an enormous impact everywhere', especially in areas of major poverty and neglect. Similarly, he points out that the next Royal Coronation will reveal what this nation really believes. The last was Protestant Christian in a way that he believes the state would not go through with today, so it begs the question 'What will it be that we will believe? We will at least believe something. Without believing something I think society is just a howling wilderness.'

He calls politics an arena that is 'increasingly secular and God-hating'. For Christians going into politics, Peter is blunt: 'They are going to be reviled. Therefore, the question when you do that will be what issues you choose to do it on, how you express those principles, and indeed whether you got them right!'

This expectation that we will be despised is tough, but it is there in the Beatitudes (Matthew 5:10–12) and throughout the Bible. In Peter's opinion: 'Once you have ... decided to speak, I think you have to take it as a compliment that you are being surrounded by howls of execration and being hosed down with slime.' From Bible-burning atheism to being hosed with rhetorical slime, Peter Hitchens is never *not* radical.

6

Because we need to show up and sit at the table

When you canvass voters around election time, you meet all sorts of interesting people and hear their different viewpoints. There is a delicious irony in knocking on the door of a Jehovah's Witness, rather than having one of them knocking on yours! Jehovah's Witnesses (JWs) do not vote or get involved in politics. They believe that they must remain separate from earthly politics because they represent God's kingdom, and that by staying politically neutral they can better proclaim the good news to all.[1]

An edition of *The Watchtower*, the well-known magazine published by the Jehovah's Witnesses, has this to say:

> There are many reasons why God tells us to be neutral. One reason is that we imitate Jesus, who was 'no part of the world.' He never took sides in politics or in wars. (John 6:15; 17:16) Another reason is that we support God's Kingdom. Because we do not support human governments, we have a clean conscience when we preach that only God's Kingdom will solve all mankind's problems.[2]

We disagree with the JWs on this matter, as we do, more fundamentally, on the identity of Jesus Christ. And it is not just Jehovah's

---

1 For more information see <www.jw.org/en/jehovahs-witnesses/faq/political-neutrality> (accessed 6 October 2020).

2 <www.jw.org/en/library/magazines/watchtower-simplified-april-2016/maintain-neutrality-in-a-divided-world> (accessed 21 March 2022).

Witnesses who perceive politics as too ungodly, mucky, dull or irrelevant – or simply too time-consuming – to engage with. When you work in the political sphere, it's not uncommon to be cut off from having a conversation by someone explaining to you that they 'don't do politics'. Perhaps we smile politely and change the subject. But our response should probably be: 'Maybe not, but politics does you!'

Politics is essentially about how human beings organize their societies. It is the process of deciding how a country's resources are divided, how we are kept safe, how much tax we pay, what kinds of public services we receive, how we trade our goods and when we go to war.

At a very basic level, politics matters to each one of us because every decision taken by someone else will have an impact on our own lives. We may pride ourselves on staying pure and separate from this mucky world, but we still need to organize our society, and Christians are also flawed and disagree with one another. Even when the West was known as 'Christendom' over many centuries, we would hardly say that the rulers were Christlike in their exercise of power. Religion often became subservient to political ends.

We should seek to avoid the trap of looking to a political system or leader for all the answers. But if we believe that certain values should be represented in government, and yet we fail to promote or support those values, then we will end up living under a set of rules entirely defined by others.

History has always been made by those who show up and make the decisions. If Christians do not show up – if we don't get involved in the business of organizing and running our society, working for positive change in the world as God's witnesses – you can bet that other people will. And some of them will undoubtedly be seeking to promote values and priorities that we disagree with.

Andy Flannagan is the Executive Director of Christians in Politics, which encourages people to get stuck in to the bread and butter of politics – joining local parties, running community campaigns, and standing for their council, the devolved assemblies or the Westminster Parliament. His book, called *Those Who Show Up*, talks about the need for us to see politics as mission. He calls on Christians to reflect on the privilege that we have of 'participating with our Father in his mission of the redemption, restoration and reconciliation of all things to himself'. His basic definition of politics is 'just people serving people rather than themselves'.[3]

Andy's book, and the resources on the Christians in Politics website, are indispensable if you want to get involved in politics at an organizational level.[4] But we also want to encourage you to get engaged where you already are, serving others and seeking to make a difference in people's lives and confront the issues that you face every day.

If we choose not to show up, but to abdicate responsibility for who governs us, we are allowing those who do show up to direct the show. So who else might be showing up? First, of course, there will be plenty of people of no faith who want to make society a better place. Given the media narrative of corrupt and lazy politicians, it is easy to assume that everyone is in it for themselves or lying to us all the time. But this stereotype of politicians is as false as the general media stereotype of Christians as either wishy-washy or bigoted.

Let's look at Westminster. Unfortunately, while information is collected on MPs' age, gender, sexuality, ethnic background and educational background, the data is pretty silent on the faith of our legislators.[5] According to Muslim News, there were fifteen Muslim MPs in the 2017 Parliament.[6] The organization known as Christians in Parliament also has many MPs, peers and staff on its mailing list.

---

3 Andy Flannagan, *Those Who Show Up* (Edinburgh: Muddy Pearl, 2015), p. 199.
4 <www.christiansinpolitics.org.uk>.
5 Report by the House of Commons Library into the social background of Members of Parliament 1979–2019: <https://commonslibrary.parliament.uk/research-briefings/cbp-7483> (accessed 7 July 2022).
6 <https://commonslibrary.parliament.uk/diversity-in-the-2017-parliament> (accessed 7 July 2022).

Members of other faiths are represented, as well as overtly secularist and humanist parliamentarians. The House of Lords, controversially in these times, has seats for twenty-six bishops.

It used to be assumed that new Members of Parliament would swear their oath of allegiance to the Crown on the Bible. But a sign of the diversity of beliefs and backgrounds represented in the Westminster Parliament is that Members are now allowed to swear on any religious book they choose, or none, or to 'affirm' rather than swear an oath.

Now, this is not a bad thing. In a plural society where the general population holds a variety of beliefs, it is important that they are represented among those who make decisions on behalf of all of us.

However, many people also show up in politics who genuinely believe that faith itself is pernicious and malicious, and that it should have no place – or voice – in the public square. Of course, there is a spectrum of views on this matter, but they are underpinned by a general belief that the absence of faith is neutral, rational and tolerant.

Those who allow faith to affect the speeches they make and the positions they take are often seen as pursuing an agenda that is at best eccentric, possibly offensive and at worst even dangerous. A quick trawl on Twitter of the phrase 'religion and politics' predictably brings up statements showing a largely negative view. 'Religion and politics don't mix.' 'Keep religion out of politics.' 'Religion and politics are a toxic combination.'

Many of those expressing hostility feel threatened by faith. Members of the UK's secularist and humanist societies believe that Christians experience unfair and disproportionate religious privilege in our institutions through faith schools, bishops in the House of Lords, and religious exemptions from the Equality Act.[7] A recent

---

7   I am not personally in favour of an established church or state religion: I believe it is my duty as an MP, a Christian and a Liberal Democrat to be utterly committed to the freedom of others who hold different positions, and legislation that seeks to make someone adhere to a certain religion contrary to their choice is neither liberal nor helpful.

report by the National Secular Society states that the 'non-religious majority in the UK suffer from systemic discrimination in all areas monitored: government, education, society, and free expression'.[8] Instead, its members want all schools to be required 'to provide inclusive education with no particular religion or belief ethos'.[9] The clear implication is that a lack of religious faith automatically equals 'no particular ethos'.

But the truth is that there can be no such thing as a neutral public square. We all approach life with a particular world view and set of values. These are developed, often subconsciously, from our parents, peer groups, teachers, the media, faith groups and the culture around us. And society is formed of people with a myriad of beliefs and outlooks. Of course, atheist or secularist politicians have an ethos that they live by; they may simply not label it in the same way that Christians might.

But why are Christian views and values so often treated with suspicion? Sadly, we Christians do not always help ourselves, and can indeed come across as disapproving and intolerant. It is also true that Christians hold a diversity of beliefs within their faith and there is no homogeneous group. But, as discussed in chapter 3, there is a real religious illiteracy among non-Christians about our faith, and a general assumption that it seeks to control and straitjacket everyone. Hillary Clinton has said that many young people are leaving the church because they find it 'judgemental' and 'alienating'.[10]

More than this, religious views are generally seen by non-religious people as add-ons or private hobbies that people choose to indulge in because it makes them feel good but which can and should be set aside if they are likely to have a bearing on their public actions or

---

8 National Secular Society, *Faith-Shaped Holes: How religious privilege is undermining equality law*, October 2020, p. 4: <www.secularism.org.uk/uploads/download-the-full-report.pdf?v=1601058434> (accessed 7 July 2022).

9 National Secular Society, *Faith-Shaped Holes*, p. 13.

10 <https://premierchristian.news/en/news/article/hillary-clinton-young-people-reject-christianity-because-it-s-judgemental-and-alienating?_psrc=personyzePopularArticles> (accessed 7 July 2022).

pronouncements. There is little understanding of faith permeating someone's entire being, or of the freedom, grace and self-giving love that Jesus offers. 'Neutral', 'secular' or 'atheist' outlooks are simply *assumed* to be more tolerant and rational – essential qualities for twenty-first-century society.

Krish Kandiah founded Home for Good, a charity seeking to find loving homes for children in care, and he continues to work for the vulnerable in partnership with government and the third sector. His years of work with local authorities and civil servants led him to write a book called *Faitheism*, which encourages Christians and atheists to confront their perceptions of one another and to seek to understand one another better. He runs training sessions for public servants to help challenge faith biases:

> I ask delegates what they associate with three different groups of people. The first is 'Christian', the second 'Muslim' and the third 'Atheist'. Everyone in the room is university educated. Everyone has been through a rigorous selection process, and they have all received extensive training on inclusion and diversity. Nevertheless, group feedback shows that the over-whelming majority of the words associated with Christians are negative: 'Bible-basher', 'intolerant', 'bigot', 'homophobic' are just a few. Sadly the words associated with Muslims are worse: 'jihadi', 'terrorist', 'suicide bomber'. The words associated with Atheists as a group were far more positive: 'discerning', 'thoughtful' and 'rational'.[11]

This is a pretty damning view of faith and those who hold it, and it is deeply sad that people do not associate Christians with words like 'loving', 'compassionate' and 'self-giving'. Encouragingly, there is some evidence that the Covid-19 pandemic has changed the views of

---

11 Krish Kandiah, *Faitheism: Why Christians and atheists have more in common than you think* (London: Hodder & Stoughton, 2018), p. 29.

many public officials in a positive way as they worked closely with churches and faith communities to support local communities.[12] But it is because of this generally negative perception that Christians are often encouraged to leave their faith at the door when engaging in public debate.

However, even if that were possible, why would it be desirable? Christians need to demonstrate God's love in the way we engage in public debate, and to dispel some of these myths rather than hide away. We should not want our policymakers to be empty-headed and value-free. They should be able to feel comfortable with expressing their views – and defending those views – in robust but respectful debate.

We need to be clear that there is no such thing as neutrality. Everyone who shows up in politics has a world view and an agenda that he or she is seeking to pursue. But neither is this an argument to engage in politics – in order to 'stop the rot' that we think we may see in society – by making a belligerent case for our own perspective. Contrary to popular belief, most people engage in politics out of a desire to build a better community.

Unfortunately, recent developments have encouraged another set of people to show up in greater numbers: people who are keen to fight what the media call the 'culture wars'. The UK, USA and Western societies in general have become increasingly polarized, and the battle lines have been redrawn away from traditional left–right politics. Society has become far more liberal in terms of race, sexuality and gender but, as Kenan Malik wrote in *The Guardian*:

> Culture and identity play a bigger role in how we define our-selves politically. The frameworks through which we make sense

---

12 The *Keeping the Faith* report was commissioned by the All-Party Parliamentary Group on Faith and Society in 2021 and found that local councils had increased their partnerships with faith groups during the pandemic, and 91% described their experi-ence with faith groups as 'very positive' or 'positive': <www.faithandsociety.org/news/2021/02/recent-appg-report-and-faith-covenant-both-endorsed-in-parliamentary-debate> (accessed 7 July 2022).

of the world are as often 'white' or 'Muslim' or 'European' as they are 'liberal' or 'conservative' or 'socialist'. And when people talk of 'liberal' or 'conservative' – or 'Remain' or 'Leave' – these are seen as cultural identities as much as political viewpoints.[13]

People have hunkered down into these tribes, and Twitter is full of insults traded between 'woke snowflakes' and 'bigoted populists'. Universities have made headlines for 'cancelling' and 'no-platforming' speakers, as they seek to create 'safe spaces' for students not wanting to hear views that they find offensive. But how have we got into this situation where we no longer seem to be able to disagree well with one another? Boris Johnson's election victory in 2019 has been explained partly by the fact that a raft of traditional Labour seats in the north of England turned blue because voters felt neglected by two decades of emphasis on the importance of university education, immigration and globalization. The UK has divided into what David Goodhart, in his book *The Road to Somewhere*, calls 'Anywheres' and 'Somewheres': those who move around in their education and careers, and pride themselves on being tolerant, open-minded and internationalist, versus those who feel more settled in a particular place, rooted in their local community and traditions.

Philosopher Jonathan Haidt believes that these two groups not only have a different outlook on life but also tend to have very different moral foundations, which make it difficult for each to understand the other's perspective. Those who are more 'Anywhere'-oriented may define themselves as being on the progressive left of politics, and stress the value of government policies that demonstrate care (as opposed to harm), liberty (over oppression), and fairness or justice. The 'Somewhere' people place more weight on foundations of loyalty, authority and sanctity, which their opponents, who tend to believe that rules and traditions can be unjust and oppressive,

---

13 <www.theguardian.com/commentisfree/2020/jun/21/culture-wars-risk-blinding-us-to-just-how-liberal-weve-become-in-the-past-decades> (accessed 7 July 2022).

struggle to recognize as holding any form of moral basis. This is a convincing interpretation of why our country feels so divided at the moment, and why many of those showing up in public debate often seem unable to comprehend any opposing viewpoint.

One other important point about the so-called culture wars is that everyone is ascribed a package of beliefs to which they are expected to conform. Most Christians won't fit neatly into one side or other, but tend to be labelled as belonging to one group, and are then expected to hold all the beliefs that this group is supposed to follow. For example, politically liberal politicians cause consternation in their own camp if they happen to hold more socially conservative views than are acceptable within that group. Dr Lisa Cameron, an MP for the Scottish Nationalist Party (SNP), has spoken of the hurtful backlash she received from her own party when she voted against the extension of UK abortion laws into Northern Ireland.[14]

Perhaps the key to engaging in the culture wars is to decline to engage. We do not have to subscribe to this view that reduces everyone to 'us versus them', and neither do we have to get involved with the name-calling and mud-slinging. Jesus could be combative in his language, but he was not vicious; he certainly got angry at times, but he was also full of compassion. In Colossians 4:6 we are told to let our conversations 'always be full of grace, seasoned with salt'. We can be provocative, but we should also be polite.

To conclude, politics is the means of organizing our society. It affects each one of us, whether we choose to make our voice heard in the process or not. If we choose not to, then others will show up to make the decisions on our behalf. They will mostly be very genuine and passionate in their beliefs, but they may assume that an absence of faith is a neutral and objective position. They may also be fighting for one side or other of the 'culture wars' that are currently dividing the UK.

---

14 A Mucky Business podcast, episode 15, Premier Radio.

Ultimately, if Christians decide not to show up in the public square because we feel that our views are unwelcome or the whole process is simply too mucky, then faith perspectives will lose their seat at the table. Instead, we should not duck the opportunity to show that Christians are *not* abusive and graceless, and that our faith is *not* weird or awful, but that our belief in Jesus, and our desire to show his love and compassion, drive us to seek the best for our society.

As we navigate through the third decade of the twenty-first century, the UK still has a plural public square where different voices can be heard. Christian voices need to be part of the cacophony.

Case study: Marsha de Cordova

Marsha de Cordova, Labour MP for Battersea, grew up knowing that she 'wanted to make a difference'. She went to Sunday school but didn't have a relationship with God.

Marsha never aspired to have a career in politics, but has always carried a burning desire to fight injustice in the world around her. She remembers being given a book for her tenth birthday about Nelson Mandela and his use of politics and campaigning to fight the evil of apartheid, which had a profound impact on her when she was growing up.

Marsha's own experiences of injustice also fuelled and informed this desire for change. Marsha was born with nystagmus, a condition that causes involuntary eye movement. As a result, she is severely visually impaired, and is registered blind.

Marsha's mum, who brought Marsha and her siblings up in social housing, warned her from a young age that she would need to work twice as hard as everyone else to get by in a society that is hostile and often inaccessible to disabled and black people.

As a young woman, she walked into a Christian bookshop in south London one day and bought a King James Bible. She kept getting invites to her friends' churches and started going along to one to learn more. She eventually gave her life to Christ.

Jesus' willingness to lead by serving his own disciples resonated as the perfect example of how to exercise leadership. She also saw the commandments for God's people to fight injustice where they saw it, and a particular command stood out: 'Speak up for those who cannot speak for themselves, for the rights of all who are destitute...' (Proverbs 31:8). Marsha now knows that her 'purpose in life is about being the voice for the voiceless', as the verse commands.

It was this calling, she says, that 'thrust' her into a commitment to politics. She initially served as a local councillor in Lambeth, where she lived and worked. Then the 2017 snap election came. She threw her hat in the ring for a seat deemed 'unwinnable' for Labour – a seat where she was not even the candidate at the time the election was called – before overturning an 8,000-vote majority and winning.

The win seemed so unlikely that she 'genuinely believe[s] it was God-breathed' and a call from the Lord into public service.

Parliament is a particularly difficult place to navigate for disabled people. The parliamentary estate is a hotchpotch of old and new buildings with limited light, steep stairs, and a lack of ramps and other standard accessibility features. Being a black female MP has also had its challenges. Marsha has spoken out about the humiliation of being mistaken for other black female colleagues in Parliament. She has been extremely vocal about deep-rooted issues of racism and discrimination in society.

In her short period in Parliament, she has served as Labour's Shadow Secretary of State for Women and Equalities and was previously the Shadow Minister for Disabled People.

She continues to serve Battersea, campaigning on issues of economic and social justice locally, nationally and internationally, and will carry on, she says, for as long as the Lord wants her to.

7

Because God's kingdom is physical as well as spiritual

Simeon of Stylites was a fifth-century hermit who famously spent thirty-seven years sitting on top of a pillar in the Syrian desert in order to escape the distraction of society. This sounds enormously uncomfortable, but he used the practice to seek a closer relationship with God, and his example was emulated by fellow ascetics right up until the nineteenth century in Russia.

Looking at the world around us today, and the daily gloom and chaos reported in the news, it is tempting to follow Simeon's example and retreat, perhaps not up a pillar but into our own church communities. Indeed, there is a historical precedent for Christians doing exactly this, withdrawing from the mucky business of the world to concentrate on the salvation of souls and our own walk with God. It often feels that we have absorbed not only our society's belief that faith should be private and personal, but also its shuddering distaste for politics, which the news media daily exposes as – to quote George Orwell – 'a mass of lies, evasions, folly, hatred and schizophrenia'.[1]

But what are the origins of this view that Christians should withdraw from the affairs of the world? We can find its roots in the ancient Greek notion, expounded by Plato, of the soul and body as distinct entities. St Augustine was greatly influenced by Plato's philosophy, and his views in turn have been used to visualize church and state as two distinctive realms or jurisdictions: the earthly city is

---

1 George Orwell, *All Art Is Propaganda: Critical essays* (1941): <www.goodreads.com/quotes/6425343-in-our-age-there-is-no-such-thing-as-keeping> (accessed 7 July 2022).

dominated by self-interest and power-seeking, while the heavenly city revolves around the eternal love of God.

Following the crackdown of the ruling authorities on radical 'Nonconformist' Christian groups after the English Civil War in the seventeenth century and the emergence of Enlightenment secularism from the eighteenth century onwards, the belief became entrenched in the Western mindset that faith and reason are opposites, and that religion is harmful to the onward march of scientific progress and discovery. All rational people were meant to agree that faith perspectives should not be used to influence political decisions or actions.

In fact, so deeply have we imbibed this view of the world that having a faith is now seen as something to be ashamed of in UK politics. We all subconsciously recognize this. In the words of Tom Wright:

> the Enlightenment banished God into the private sphere, like a demented elderly relative confined to the attic: we can visit him from time to time, but he mustn't be allowed to come down and embarrass us, especially when there are visitors present.[2]

In addition, religion is increasingly viewed today – with some justification – as authoritarian and fundamentalist, often violent and oppressive. The last two decades have witnessed the rise of militant Islam, the 9/11 attacks, al-Qaeda and ISIS; religious nationalism in places such as France, Turkey and India; growing Christian nationalism in the USA and Russia, as well as the tarnished reputation of some disreputable television evangelists, and a series of abuse scandals covered up within the UK church that serve to confirm to many people that Christians are more concerned with protecting the church's power and reputation than witnessing to the gospel of Christ.

---

2 Tom Wright, *God in Public* (London: SPCK, 2016), p. 3.

There are also other factors at work causing the unpopularity of faith views in society. Traditional value systems and structures of external authority have been challenged by deep-seated social and cultural changes that began in the 1960s, which – while bringing about many positive changes – also saw the growth of a radical individualism that, according to psychiatrist and author Glynn Harrison, has 'heighten[ed] the sovereignty of the individual over all other sources of authority'.[3] Alongside this has been a rise in muscular secularism, which actively seeks to weed out any form of religious 'privilege' from society, for example in banning the hijab in France or campaigning against overt demonstrations of faith in public life in the UK. Today's acceptable notion of 'spirituality' expresses the Gnostic idea that we all have a divine spark within us, which we are free to seek as part of our own private spiritual journeys.

Identity politics and national populism are also on the rise. Tom Wright sees the roots of these movements in the consequences of empire, where rich and powerful people were in charge and ordinary folk could not affect decisions that were being made on their behalf. This led to decades of political apathy which *perhaps* led to the 2016 Brexit vote and the subsequent capture by the Conservatives of the 'red wall' of traditional Labour-voting seats in the north of England in 2019. All of this could be seen as an uprising against the 'tyranny of merit'. This is philosopher Michael Sandel's phrase to describe the relentless ethic of success arising from an individualism that believed '[t]hose at the top [of society] deserved their place but so too did those who were left behind [because they] hadn't striven as effectively'.[4]

The forces of national populism have spearheaded this awakening. They can be seen in organizations such as the UK Brexit Party,

---

3 Glynn Harrison, *A Better Story: God, sex and human flourishing* (London: IVP, 2017), p. 11.
4 <www.theguardian.com/books/2020/sep/06/michael-sandel-the-populist-backlash-has-been-a-revolt-against-the-tyranny-of-merit> (accessed 7 July 2022).

renamed Reform UK, which, despite Brexit 'being done', came third in the Old Bexley and Sidcup by-election in December 2021. They appeal to many who previously did not bother to engage in politics by 'prioritis[ing] the culture and interests of the nation, and . . . promis[ing] to give voice to a people who feel that they have been neglected, even held in contempt, by distant and often corrupt elites'.[5] The UK of the 2020s faces increasing polarization as rival groups gather around their identities and entrench themselves against one another.

The Covid-19 pandemic, while initially uniting the nation around the NHS and the goal of keeping everyone safe, soon began to cause signs of strain as the elites and middle classes were perceived to be able to ride out the lockdowns while the disadvantaged increasingly struggled. Then, in late 2021 and early 2022, trust in politics and politicians was further undermined by the 'Partygate' scandal.[6] Evidence emerged of the repeated violation of Covid lockdown rules by Boris Johnson and those in Number 10 – the very people who had set the rules for the rest of the country. They were discovered to have been holding frequent social gatherings at times when everyone else was banned from socializing or even visiting dying relatives, and then to be denying and defending their actions. Politics began to feel even more dishonest and broken.

Of course, all this is a simplification of the different factors at work, which have yet to be fully played out, but it offers a brief summary of what is going on in our political system. And indeed, why on earth should Christians want to get involved in trying to untangle all of this? Evangelical branches of the church have tended to focus on eternal salvation, through which we can look forward to

---

5 Roger Eatwell and Matthew Goodwin, *National Populism: The revolt against liberal democracy* (London: Penguin, 2018), p. 48.

6 For some background and guidance on a Christian response, see: <https://ivpbooks.com/blog/what-should-christians-learn-about-leadership-from-boris-johnson-s-partygate.html> (accessed 7 July 2022).

escaping this world to heaven where all this division and hurt will be a distant memory.

However, this focus can lead to a powerful misconception. For example, here is a common explanation for how Christians should respond to politics, in this case from the popular conservative Christian US website Got Questions, which seeks to present prayerful and Bible-based answers to Christians' and sceptics' questions about faith:

> Nowhere in Scripture do we have the directive to spend our energy, our time, or our money in governmental affairs. Our mission lies not in changing the nation through political reform, but in changing hearts through the Word of God. When believers think the growth and influence of Christ can somehow be allied with government policy, they corrupt the mission of the church. Our Christian mandate is to spread the gospel of Christ and to preach against the sins of our time. Only as the hearts of individuals in a culture are changed by Christ will the culture begin to reflect that change.[7]

There are two main points being made here. The first is that we can't look to politicians, ideologies or systems of government to save our souls or our nations. The second is that the church as the collective body of Christ has a primary mandate to deliver on the Great Commission of Matthew 28, to 'go and make disciples of all nations'.

These observations both make a lot of sense at first sight. No human ideology holds all the answers to solving the world's problems. We certainly should not expect our governments to bring about human salvation. The Bible is clear that only Jesus can do this. And he has called us to tell others the good news. Also, in the USA there is a far closer link than in the UK between specific political

---

7 <www.gotquestions.org/Christian-politics.html> (accessed 7 July 2022).

movements and Christian groups seeking to gain political power through them.

But the danger lies when we use these assumptions to convince ourselves that we have no business getting involved in politics to tackle the poverty, hunger and injustice that are rife in our world. Jesus said we will always have the poor with us, but he didn't mean us to accept this fact, shrug, and leave it at that.

And this is where that alleged dichotomy between body and soul again becomes a hindrance. The American former political adviser Charles Colson said of the evangelical church: 'Our movement's great strength – and yet also its weakness – is defining faith in terms of personal salvation alone ... it has ... made soul-winning an end in itself.' But he cautions: 'we are not only saved *from* sin, we are also saved *to* something: to the task of developing God's creation.'[8]

God commanded humans to carry on his creative work, filling and subduing the earth:

> this is the 'cultural commission' and it is just as binding as the Great Commission. It means we must go beyond personal conversion and develop a faith that encompasses every part of life – every sphere of work, every aspect of the world.[9]

God's kingdom is physical as well as spiritual.

Yes, Jesus came to save souls. He also reached and changed people's hearts by practical means. He healed them and fed them and cared for their bodies as well. He hungered for justice. Indeed, justice runs as a major thread through the Bible and we see that God expects his people to enact it. For example, we see in the book of Isaiah that

> [t]he LORD looked and was displeased
>   that there was no justice.

---

8   Charles Colson, 'What are we doing here?' *Christianity Today*, 4 October 1999.
9   Colson, 'What are we doing here?'

He saw that there was no one,
  he was appalled that there was no one
    to intervene . . .
(Isaiah 59:15–16)

The Old Testament 'Books of the Law' are full of commands to ensure that God's people did not take advantage of one another but acted generously in supporting one another, looking after the widows, orphans and foreigners among them.

Now of course, in reality, today's church at all levels is extremely involved in practical measures to tackle these evils. Church communities have stepped into the gap left by the state to run food banks and provide debt counselling and other services at the heart of their neighbourhoods. This is the outworking of God's love for his people. But we are wary of labelling these actions as 'politics', and certain sections of the church are anxious about the promotion of the 'social gospel' for fear of emphasizing physical needs at the cost of watering down the gospel and compromising with the values of the world. A divide has been established between those who think of the church's role as otherworldly and those whose faith is grounded in the gritty reality of local communities.

But this is a false divide. Before we realize that future hope promised in the Bible, where there will be no more death or suffering, pain or corruption, we must live out our lives in a fallen world with other fallen humans. All walks of life can be mucky. All jobs have their challenges. And if we retreat, hermit-like, we are in fact abdicating some of our God-given responsibilities. We will talk more about this in the next chapter.

The Bible is clear that God gives authority to human rulers and structures. Paul in Romans 13:1 says: 'Let everyone be subject to the governing authorities, for there is no authority except that which God has established. The authorities that exist have been established by God.' But the Canadian-American philosopher James K. A. Smith refutes the idea that this means we can therefore sit back and let others take all the decisions:

> The church is not a soul-rescue depot that leaves us to muddle through the regrettable earthly burden of 'politics' ... the church is a body politic that invites us to imagine how politics could be otherwise. And we are sent from worship to be Christ's image-bearers to and for our neighbours, which includes the ongoing creaturely stewardship and responsibility to order the social world in ways that are conducive to flourishing but particularly attentive to the vulnerable – the widows, orphans, and strangers in our midst.[10]

He is clear that politics falls within the scope of 'all things' that Christ creates, redeems and rules. And God has inspired many of his people over the centuries to carry out his work. William Wilberforce is the poster boy of Christian political involvement. God used him, and many others around him whose names we are less familiar with, to bring about the abolition of the slave trade through political reform.

The Bible also tells us that we have a duty to seek the common good of our society: 'Seek the welfare of the city where I have sent you into exile, and pray to the LORD on its behalf, for in its welfare you will find your welfare' (Jeremiah 29:7 ESV). The early Christians whose stories are told in the book of Acts came together to ensure that they '[gave] to anyone who had need'. And, *as part of the same process*, 'the Lord added to their number daily those who were being saved' (Acts 2:45, 47).

One more point should be made about the consequences of thinking of the spiritual realm and earthly realm as separate, and

---

10 James K. A. Smith, *Awaiting the King: Reforming public theology* (Grand Rapids, MI: Baker Academic, 2017), p. 16.

this perhaps holds the fundamental key to why Christians get involved in politics.

To those of us who believe that we will be 'going to heaven when we die', books such as James Paul's *What on Earth Is Heaven?* or Tom Wright's meaty *Surprised by Hope* are quite a revelation. They refute the general view held by many Christians today about what 'heaven' actually looks like in the Bible. James Paul states: 'Many of the things we think we know about heaven are half-baked versions of the truth, influenced more by ancient philosophies, the medieval imagination and pop culture than by what the Bible actually says.'[11]

In fact, he points out:

Nowhere in the Bible does it say that heaven is an escape route through which we flee from the imperfections of our earthly lives. Rather, the Bible tells the story of a God who never gives up on his earthly creation . . . God's plan at the end of time is not to destroy the world he has made but to redeem it, and rather than people escaping the earth for heaven, the Bible talks about the kingdom of heaven coming to earth.[12]

Instead of telling us to grit our teeth and endure this world until we can escape elsewhere, the Bible talks of the creation of a new heaven *and a new earth*, which will ultimately be joined together. Through Jesus' death and resurrection, we see that God has chosen not to withdraw from the mess that his human creation has made, but to break into it, and to act from within the world to put it to rights.

And he asks us to work alongside him in this, to reflect him into his world, to carry out acts of mercy and justice and to draw people to him as part of this process.

This is a joyful, revolutionary hope that what we do now really does echo in eternity. It turns the idea of escaping to heaven

11 James Paul, *What on Earth Is Heaven?* (London: IVP, 2021), p. 5.
12 Paul, *What on Earth Is Heaven?*, p. 5.

completely on its head. We are not called to hide away. God's kingdom is physical, not just spiritual. He came to earth as a human being to redeem it from within. We are not seeking salvation *from* the earth but *of* it. Jesus rolled up his sleeves and washed the disciples' feet, and he promises one day to complete the process of redemption, not just of individuals but of all creation.

There is so much more to be said on this issue, but another of Tom Wright's books, *God in Public*, sums it up thus:

This is the strange public truth of the Christian gospel. God is in the business of remaking the whole world, turning it the right way up at last. The call of the Christian gospel makes the sense it's supposed to make, not when it is heard as a call to ignore the world and pursue a private salvation, but when it is heard as a call to follow Jesus and become part of his plan to sort out the world now, as much as we can, in advance of the final day.[13]

Case study: Paul Boateng

Lord Paul Boateng has had a remarkable career as a lawyer and a politician in both chambers of Parliament, as the UK's first cabinet minister of African descent and as a Methodist lay preacher. His upbringing and experiences in early life were formative for the two great callings on his life: his faith and his politics.

His parents were both committed Christians and committed activists for colonial freedom. He was profoundly influenced by growing up in newly independent Ghana where his mother was a renowned teacher and his father was a lawyer and cabinet minister before his arrest and imprisonment without trial. He was then forced to flee to the UK with his mother and sister, where he

---

13 Wright, *God in Public*, p. 111.

found himself the only black boy in his school and on the council estate in Hemel Hempstead where the family lived. This was in the late 1960s – a 'very political time, with the civil rights struggle in the US, and the anti-apartheid movement in the UK'. His school had a culture of friendly political debate, and even the local pub held Friday night debates upstairs.

All of these experiences formed Paul's political outlook as a result of his Christian faith, because it was 'a faith that believes in active engagement'. It led initially to a career as a lawyer and into his 'vocation' in politics as an MP and a key figure in the New Labour governments. But on party politics he is firm – no one party or ideology is more Christian than others, and 'our calling to follow Christ leads one in many different directions'.

There are, however, non-negotiables for Christians in politics. 'I think if you are a Christian, you have to be engaged in making a difference in our world and in the life of others. But I don't believe a vote ever brings closer the coming of the kingdom of heaven.'

In politics we must get stuck in to the concrete realities of this world: 'I find a constant joy and solace, but also a spur to action, in God's love.' That action for him looks like loving the neighbours we may never meet – the world's poor. Right now, that means working for global vaccine equality, and getting involved in all the detailed ways in which developing countries can be allowed to manufacture their own vaccines. Vaccination rates in the non-Western world are still very low, and the Covid-19 pandemic will not be over until the vaccine and the facilities needed to produce it can be properly and generously shared.

We can expect trouble. The examples of Shadrach, Meshach and Abednego, and of Daniel in the lions' den, show that politics can be 'deeply corrosive'. In politics, as in any calling, 'you've got to hold on to God's love and what is right'. Lord Paul lastly points to the rousing words of an old spiritual song for encouragement:

Dare to be a Daniel,
Dare to stand alone,
Dare to have a purpose firm,
Dare to make it known![14]

---

14 From the hymn 'Standing by a purpose true' by P. P. Bliss, 1873.

8

Because Jesus didn't turn away but broke his heart for us

It's been in the background since the beginning of this book, but in the last chapter we started digging in to one of the key aspects of political action: social justice. Many Christians who have grown up in conservative evangelical circles might define themselves as hard-line social justice cynics. Social justice is often perceived as window dressing for theological liberalism; code for a cuddly Christianity that has moved away from the truth of the gospel, and the need to proclaim it, in favour of seeking popularity and the approval of the world. Clearly, the thinking goes, these liberal Christians don't realize that what people really need is to turn to Jesus and put their faith in him. What good are food, clothing and rights in the here and now, if our lives on earth are like the brief life cycle of grass? There is a suspicion that 'social justice Christians' don't have a thorough enough understanding of Scripture and just want to be liked by the people around them.

This harsh characterization may be true of some, but it's just as likely that, if you speak to Christians who emphasize the importance of social justice, you may find that they have had their heart broken somehow, perhaps merely by watching a hard-hitting TV programme or encountering someone's powerful story of struggling. Sometimes our hearts aren't broken in a moment but over time, so slowly that we don't even really notice it happening until we realize we now hold convictions that two years ago we would have scoffed at. So if you are curious, indifferent or even the most hardened cynic when it comes to the need for Christian political engagement and social justice, please read on, because heartbreak is not just important; it is essential. You will find it difficult to care otherwise.

What does it mean to get your heart broken? Unsurprisingly, we are not talking about romantic heartbreak. At its core it is heartbreak at a broken world; heartbreak at the state of humanity, the injustice and suffering, the damage we do to one another and our planet. These are all things we know. There is nothing like a global pandemic and its consequences to bring home the brokenness of the world. Many of us will have experienced this personally. Heartbreak starts the same way as Jesus did: by entering into the mess. When we engage in the pain and suffering in people's lives, we will often uncover the social injustices that lie beneath them. The chances are we won't have to look very far.

One of the big misconceptions we have is that caring about social justice isn't as difficult as evangelism. But that isn't actually the case. To really engage with people, with their lives, concerns and needs, is incredibly costly. We all know that it is the people we love the most, and invest in the most, who are capable of causing us the most pain. Jesus demonstrated this while he was here on earth. His pain at the death of his dearly loved friend Lazarus shows the cost of love in our fallen world. The power of the shortest verse in the Bible, 'Jesus wept' (John 11:35), has had a profound impact on readers throughout the centuries.

God's grace, mercy and love for his people are displayed over and over again in both the Old and New Testaments. And who knows better than God that each act of generosity and mercy will once again end in disobedience and rejection?

God's love for humanity, for those who rejected him, for his people Israel and his people the church, leaves him vulnerable to deep hurt. This is shown powerfully and heartbreakingly in the book of Hosea. Israel is pictured as an adulterous wife returning to her lovers over and over again, and God as the husband who continues to take her back. In Hosea 11:1–4, God's love for his people is also compared to the love of a father for his child:

When Israel was a child, I loved him,
　　and out of Egypt I called my son.
But the more they were called,
　　the more they went away from me.
They sacrificed to the Baals
　　and they burned incense to images.
It was I who taught Ephraim to walk,
　　taking them by the arms;
but they did not realise
　　it was I who healed them.
I led them with cords of human kindness,
　　with ties of love.
To them I was like one who lifts
　　a little child to the cheek,
　　and I bent down to feed them.

The Bible makes it clear that we do not have a disengaged and distant heavenly Father, but rather a God who is intimately concerned with the whole of our lives. Disengagement, and even disinterest, is a privilege. Many of us live a comfortable middle-class life, where most of the deep injustices in society and across the world do not confront us on a daily basis, or even a weekly or monthly basis. The news may be the closest we get. Of course, that won't be the case for everyone reading this book. In fact, in the wake of Covid-19 and the cost-of-living crisis, society's injustices may be brought closer to home. But stop for a minute and consider the composition of your church family. If our churches were full of the poorest in our communities, issues around the provision of social housing or the level of universal credit would be far nearer the top of our agenda. If they are issues we don't feel we have to confront as a church, that is a symptom of the fact that our church doesn't accurately represent the breadth of our society.

But why is it so important that we engage with these issues? Surely people's eternal salvation is far more important, and sharing the gospel is what loving them really looks like? And if the broken world will remain broken until the new creation, shouldn't all our energy be spent on securing people's eternity? There are a number of crucial reasons why this view is flawed.

Most fundamentally, we need to understand something of the character of the God we worship, the God who calls us to follow him. Passages such as the powerful redemptive narrative in the book of Hosea give us a taste of the concept discussed in the last chapter, that God's kingdom is physical as well as spiritual. And in Jesus' life we see the practical applications of it. Jesus' compassion for people, for both their physical and spiritual needs, is littered throughout the Gospels. The three accounts of the feeding of the five thousand in Matthew, Mark and John bring this into sharp focus. Jesus is hungry and exhausted and has just heard news of his cousin's murder. He and his disciples retreat for some respite:

> But many who saw them leaving recognised them and ran on foot from all the towns and got there ahead of them. When Jesus landed and saw a large crowd, he had compassion on them, because they were like sheep without a shepherd.
> (Mark 6:33–34a)

The above may be a familiar verse, but consider the context of a grieving, hungry and exhausted man. Most of us would have thought Jesus reasonable if he had excused himself for a few days, sent the crowd away, or simply just broken down and wept. The depth of compassion that our Saviour has for these people is incredibly humbling and slightly mind-blowing. Notably, the different Gospel accounts pick up on different aspects of Jesus' compassionate response. In Mark we read, 'So he began to teach them many things' (6:34b), in Matthew that 'he had compassion on them and healed their sick' (14:14). Jesus' compassion leads him to address both the physical and spiritual needs of the people. We see this all the more as the story plays out and Jesus provides for their most basic physical need: food. These are people who, according to John, are following him because of the signs and miracles they have seen him perform, not because they have any faith in him as the Messiah. Just this one very familiar miracle reveals the depth of compassion our Saviour has, a compassion that expresses itself in addressing people's spiritual *and* physical needs.

I don't know if you have ever been in a church service where the speaker is discussing repentance and uses the illustration of an army officer commanding troops. The officer calls 'REPENT!' and the soldiers do an about-turn – 180 degrees. The point of the illustration is that when we turn to follow Jesus, it is a complete life-change. It may not be the most emotive illustration, but it does demonstrate the totality of change that takes place. The entirety of our lives has changed direction. We are following a shepherd who gave everything for his sheep. To suggest that this should result in negligence of people's physical needs makes absolutely no sense. God created people in their entirety, including their physical needs, and he cares about those needs. As we cry out in the face of illness and suffering, we rejoice in knowing that God sees us and cares for us.

In Tim Chester's excellent book *Good News to the Poor*, he references *Justice, Mercy and Humility: Integral mission and the poor* by Gary Haugen, the president of International Justice Mission (IJM). As he considers the story of the good Samaritan, Haugen calls on the reader to consider what love requires. He follows this by telling the stories of some of the people IJM has worked with. Here is one of them:

Joyti is a 14-year-old girl from a rural town in India who was abducted and drugged by four women who sold her into a brothel in Bombay. She was locked away in an underground cell and severely beaten with metal rods, plastic pipe and electrical cord until submitting to provide sex to the customers. Now she must work 7 days a week, servicing 20–40 customers a day.[1]

This is an utterly heartbreaking story that should make us sick to our stomach. So, what does love require? As Chester states:

> Love certainly does require that the gospel is proclaimed to Joyti, to her oppressors and to her customers. But does that exhaust our obligation of love towards her? What does love require? 'Dear children, let us not love with words or tongue but with actions and in truth' (1 John 3 v18).[2]

Overemphasis on evangelism, at the expense of everything else, leaves us with a hollow gospel. In his first letter, John speaks beautifully on the subject of God's love. He writes: 'This is how God showed his love among us: he sent his one and only Son into the world that we might live through him' (1 John 4:9). We are assured of God's love because he put his money where his mouth is. His love was shown in action. If we speak of love but do not act in love and compassion, how can we expect that love to be understood in any meaningful way? We tell people about a God who loves them, the God of the church, and in many cases they would be well within their rights to turn to us, both personally and collectively, and say 'How?' Christ's name is dishonoured in our hands if we preach personal morality without showing love in society. Or perhaps evangelism includes loving people practically, not just telling them the gospel? Love, friendship and care are far more costly than standing on soapboxes and sending angry

---

1   Tim Chester, *Good News to the Poor: Social involvement and the gospel* (Wheaton, IL: Crossway, 2013), p. 33.
2   Chester, *Good News to the Poor*, p. 34.

emails to your MP. The gospel is the most incredible news. We are safe, known, loved and secure for eternity if we trust in Jesus. And if that is our position, what do we have to lose? It is because we are secured for eternity that we can afford to love and give and care generously for those who are around us.

When we allow our hearts to be broken, to love the people God created, we also find in ourselves a greater longing for Christ's return and for justice to be done against the evil in our world. This is where the hope of the gospel reaches out beyond our personal salvation and embraces all of creation.

The proclamation of the gospel and our treatment of those around us are intrinsically linked. In fact, the gospel is all the more reason we *should* engage. The world and its people are physical and earthbound, and so that is how we show God's love alongside the message of the gospel. Or was Jesus just wasting his time when he healed people? Was his compassion for their hunger a waste of time?

God 'so loved the world that he gave his one and only Son, that whoever believes in him shall not perish but have eternal life' (John 3:16). We see the miracle of the eternal, infinite, pure, holy God of the universe laying aside the perfection of heaven to join a cruel, painful, heartbroken world and bring his wayward people back to himself. Why? Out of love. He loved them. He loves us. We love because he first loved us (1 John 4:19).

Case study: Pastor Mick

We should celebrate ordinary testimonies of people quietly accepting Jesus and faithfully following him for many years. But occasionally I hear a testimony like Pastor Mick Fleming's and I am newly astounded. A brief account will not do justice to his story, so I urge you to read any of the recent mainstream media profiles, and get your hands on his recent autobiography, *Blown Away: From drug dealer to life bringer.*[3] Mick also appeared in a BBC documentary that followed the work of his church over the course of the pandemic.[4] From a childhood fraught with devastating pain, grief and trauma, to a life of crime, violence and substance abuse, he was led to a dramatic encounter with God on the way to a drug-related debt-collection job.

Mick is now a pastor in his home town of Burnley, leading Church on the Street Ministries. The ministry meets the many desperate physical needs of those living in poverty nearby – providing food services (meals, breakfasts, food banks), daily drop-ins, accommodation support, addiction recovery support, mental health and medical support, benefits advice, and even funeral support.

During the pandemic, Church on the Street stepped up. Existing problems were only made worse by the crisis, and people already struggling across the UK became ever more desperate. The BBC followed Mick on his rounds on an ordinary day during the pandemic. 'The need's massive,' he says, 'absolutely colossal ... I've seen people who are working, who can't make ends meet ... I go into houses and I sometimes have children ripping the bags open to get at the food as I carry them through the door.' The role of faith groups – whether mosques, synagogues or gurdwaras – in meeting the needs of the poor only became more obvious over the course of the pandemic. Churches of all traditions were also central to this.

Yet this practical meeting of people's needs – this carrying out of Jesus' command in Matthew 25:35–36 to provide food for the hungry, water for the thirsty, clothing for the naked, care for the sick, and company for the imprisoned – received some uncharitable

---

3   Mick Fleming, *Blown Away: From drug dealer to life bringer* (London: SPCK, 2022).
4   Ed Thomas, 'Burnley's Pastor Mick – from dangerous drug dealer to lifesaver', BBC News, 18 December 20: <www.bbc.co.uk/news/stories-55273677> (accessed 9 July 2022).

criticism. While Church on the Street meets people's many physical needs, what about their spiritual needs? If the church only provides for physical needs, isn't it just an empty social gospel?

If that were the case, Mick says, they would be right. But the criticism comes from those who 'don't know me, and they don't know the work; they only know and judge from what they've seen on television. I'm not just a nice man giving out food parcels – I'm probably not a nice man anyway. It's all about telling the story of Jesus.'

He goes on: 'So if you come for a food parcel, we're going to find out what the real problem is. And all the excuses everybody's got – I don't have a suit for an interview, I can't fill the forms out, I've had nothing to eat, I've got mental health issues, I've got addiction issues – we'll take them all away, until you're stood on your own before God. And then you can make a decision.

'We're seeing people in their hundreds with lives changed, and the people from secular outside agencies are being touched and being changed.'

Beyond the charitable works and sharing the gospel, Pastor Mick is not apolitical nor disconnected. His challenge is that 'politicians try to see too big'. He uses the example of levelling up Burnley, for instance. The town will receive money from the government to expand the shopping centre in an attempt to vaguely improve the economy, while National Insurance contributions go up and the cost-of-living crisis deepens.[5] Politicians overlook the routes out of poverty grounded in the local community: 'What they fail to see is the smaller organizations that are effective.' It is these smaller organizations, such as churches, that are 'building the community that gels people together and then they break out of poverty'.

---

5 <www.cots-ministries.co.uk/blog/levelling-up-better-to-keep-our-feet-on-the-ground> (accessed 9 July 2022).

Mick also has a powerful rebuke for all politicians. 'I haven't seen many politicians who will weep with the poor. Not *for* them. Not talk good things about them. Not say nice things and write words. Will actually weep *with* them. When you get leaders ... that can and do have the ability in their hearts to weep with the poor, you'll see real change, because then the politicians will know ... it's them that's poor, and they'll realize they have a need for God in their lives, and that'll bring change. I don't see it ... too often.'

If you are involved in politics, or you want to be, pay attention.

9

Because faith is not private and Christians have always engaged

When we think about Christian 'heroes' our poster boy is often William Wilberforce (as mentioned previously). His story demonstrates how Christianity should have an essential and fundamental impact on our political being. But Wilberforce lived two hundred years ago, and we can't ride on the good works of our Christian forebears to demonstrate that our faith is still radical and relevant today. So where do we look to find current examples of Christians who can inspire us like Wilberforce?

Hebrews 11, often referred to as a 'hall of faith', recounts the stories of men and women throughout biblical history – from Abel and Sarah to Moses and Gideon – whose faith moved them to action. The same is true of Christians today. There's a reason why some names are well known within Christian circles. First, behind the names are incredible, faithful people who have prayerfully dedicated their lives to God's purpose. And second, what these people achieved through their work was often far-reaching. However, in Hebrews, the author doesn't just focus on the outcomes – he commends people for their character and faith.

William Wilberforce achieved a lot. He had a profound impact on the course of human society. The abolition of the slave trade. Pretty big stuff. If we're honest, sometimes stories of such magnitude wow us, but they can also snuff us out. We think: *I could never do anything like that . . . Oh, I'd love to, but . . .*

If we're to be truly *inspired*, we need to be 'filled with the urge and ability to do something'. (That's what the dictionary says.) We have to feel able to do it ourselves.

Let's not define a successful application to the vacancy of 'modern-day William Wilberforce' by status, scale or calculable outcomes. Let's define it by character. And to aid us, we'll coin a new term:

Wilberforcean (noun)
One who exhibits the same characteristics and traits possessed by William Wilberforce

We hope this chapter serves to inspire you in three ways. First, by helping you to see that there are magnificent testimonies of God using his people in *our* time too. We can only provide a snapshot of a few stories here. Second, by showing that you're not as far off from being a modern-day William Wilberforce as you may think. Perhaps you already are one! And, third, may this chapter inspire you to recognize and encourage those around you who express Wilberforcean qualities. Maybe one day, someone will write a book about them.

Preface over. Let's begin.

1 God's 'Great Objects'

As we emphasize throughout this book, we live in a fallen and broken world. Despite Wilberforce's best efforts, there are more people enslaved today than at any other time in history. One per cent of the world's population have been forced to flee their homes due to war or persecution. During the coronavirus pandemic, the number of people on the brink of starvation doubled to 270 million.

Justice is at the heart of the Christian faith. Timothy Keller, in *Generous Justice: How God's grace makes us just*, writes: 'If a person has grasped the meaning of God's grace in his heart, he [or she] will do justice.'[1] We set out in the previous chapter how the natural overflow of God's love is for us to see injustice and to want to fix it. However, this often means we feel a responsibility to fix *everything*. And then we question whether we're on the right path to doing that:

What if I worked for the United Nations?
Maybe I could be an MP.
Should I get a job with Tearfund?
I should move abroad.
Do I need a Master's?
Maybe I need to learn Arabic – and Spanish . . .

Unpruned, this intrinsic Christian desire can make us feel lost and confused, with the weight of the world on our shoulders. In Wilberforce's time, just as today, there was a myriad of sociopolitical challenges and injustices spanning the length and breadth of society. It would have been easy for Wilberforce to involve himself directly in every one of these and to spread himself too thin.

But here's what William Wilberforce said: 'God Almighty has set before me two Great Objects: the suppression of the Slave Trade and the Reformation of Manners.'[2] Well, that's liberating. Two things. That's it? I don't know about you, but I feel I could handle two things.

To be Wilberforcean, therefore, is to discern where God wants us to focus and to pursue those causes with intent, rather than be crippled by options.

Hope Virgo is a full-time writer, speaker and mental health campaigner who exemplifies this characteristic. She created the campaign #DumpTheScales, an initiative which seeks to change policy and practice concerning eating disorders. Pippa Gumbel describes Hope

---

1 Timothy Keller, *Generous Justice: How God's grace makes us just* (London: Hodder & Stoughton, 2010), p. 93.
2 William Wilberforce, diary entry, 28 October 1787.

as someone who has 'given her life' to making a difference to all the girls and boys, women and men, who are struggling in this area.[3]

Hope has worked tirelessly to build relationships with MPs in the Houses of Parliament, visited 10 Downing Street, and appeared on many national broadcasting outlets including the BBC and Sky News. She says, 'Campaigning is my passion and something that drives me every day to keep fighting the injustices that so many people face.'[4] It is the laser-like focus in one area that has helped generate the momentum behind Hope's campaigns.

If you're struggling to identify where God wants to send you, I find it helpful to remember the words of Hillsong's worship song 'Hosanna', asking him to break our hearts for what breaks his.[5] Make that your prayer.

2 What's in your hand?

Now, you may be thinking that the two Great Objects set before William Wilberforce would still seem pretty impossible if they were set before *you*. But Wilberforce was already an MP prior to becoming a Christian and receiving this commission. He was known for being a powerful public persuader with connections to people in places of power. God made the most of the tools that Wilberforce already possessed and the position that Wilberforce was already in.

Likewise, in Exodus 4, Moses tells God that he's picked the wrong guy to lead the Israelites out of Egypt. 'Who am I to do that?' he asks. God answers him by asking, almost comically, 'What's in your hand?' Moses had a shepherd's staff in his hand. The most ordinary, common thing – just a stick, really. A stick which led the Israelites out of Egypt.

3 Quoted in Hope Virgo, *You Are Free (Even If You Don't Feel Like It)* (London: SPCK, 2022), p. xiii.
4 Virgo, *You Are Free*, p. 5.
5 'Hosanna', words and music by Brooke Taylor: <https://hillsong.com/lyrics/hosanna> (accessed 11 July 2022).

In 2001, Tich and Joan Smith heard that children in Amaoti township – about 12 miles (20 km) from their beachfront house in Durban, South Africa – were starving and neglected. Many lived on the streets and knocked on doors asking for food. Amaoti was one of the largest informal settlements in the region, with over 100,000 residents. Unemployment was extremely high, and criminal gangs operated from the township. The scale of the problem seemed enormous.

Tich and Joan felt they had to do something, but they couldn't see a vision beyond giving out peanut butter sandwiches to a few children under a tree once a week. So that's where they started. Once a week quickly turned into once a day. The menu expanded to soup. A few children became hundreds.

Fast-forward to today and Tich and Joan have founded Lungisisa Indlela Village (LIV), which offers long-term care for orphaned and vulnerable children in small homes with a foster mother.[6] Over 170 children now call LIV 'home'. At capacity, LIV will be home to 150 mothers and 1,000 children. The model, which replicates the Watoto villages in Uganda founded by Gary and Marilyn Skinner, is catching on. The South African government has woken up to the success of LIV. The Smiths already have land in Cape Town and Johannesburg to build other villages, and their vision is for thousands across Africa.

Like Wilberforce, Tich and Joan didn't just have their hearts broken – they did something about it. Instead of being intimidated by the magnitude of injustice, they took the small offering of peanut butter sandwiches in their hands and trusted God faithfully. Looking back on the extraordinary journey which God has taken them on, Joan says: 'I am amazed at how unqualified we are to be doing this ... the only qualification we need is to be passionately in love with Jesus and say "YES" to Him.'[7]

6 <www.liv-village.com/about> (accessed 9 July 2022).
7 Tich and Joan Smith, *When Grace Showed Up: One couple's story of hope and healing among the poor* (Colorado Springs, CO: David C. Cook, 2016).

We often convince ourselves that injustice is too hard to overcome. That we're not cut out for the fight. That we need to have better qualifications, to have taken a different path. But God isn't restrained by these things. He has been preparing us all along. The question Wilberforceans ask themselves is not 'What don't I have?'; it's 'What's in my hand?' Don't panic about the finish line. Start where you are.

3 Persistence and determination

Be aware: the road to political breakthrough may be extremely long, arduous and fraught with setbacks.

Wilberforce first delivered a speech on the abolition of the slave trade in the House of Commons on 12 May 1789. Interrupted by some tactical filibustering (the deliberate prolonging of parliamentary debate to defer a vote) and a general election, he was forced to wait two years to present his first Parliamentary Bill on the matter. The first of many.

In April 1791, the Slave Trade Abolition Bill was defeated by 163 votes to 88. In 1792, it passed . . . only to be thrown out by the House of Lords. Again in 1793, 1794, 1795, 1796 – defeat, after defeat, after defeat. In 1805, Sir Banastre Tarleton proclaimed that 'ever since [Wilberforce] had a seat in Parliament we have had an annual debate on this subject'. Wilberforce's commitment to the cause was unwavering, despite frustration and hostility.

Finally, on 25 March 1807, the Slave Trade Act received royal assent and became law. By this point, Wilberforce's arguments for the abolition of the slave trade had been debated and rebuffed by many of the same people for nearly two decades.[8] The Act shattered three quarters of the British slave trade. Even then, he didn't rest until total and permanent abolition was accomplished throughout the British Empire in 1833.

---

8   William Hague, *William Wilberforce: The life of the great anti-slave trade campaigner* (London: HarperPress, 2007), ch. 13, 'Abolition'.

Wilberforce's anti-slavery quest spanned forty-two years. Imagine if he had given in to fatigue at any point. To be Wilberforcean, therefore, is to reflect his 'unwearied industry' and 'indefatigable zeal'.[9]

One person who embodies this Wilberforcean persistence is Baroness Caroline Cox, who is approaching her fortieth year in the House of Lords. She has used her position to be a voice for those whose voices aren't being heard in Nigeria, Sudan, South Sudan, Syria, Burma and – a place you may not even know exists – Nagorno-Karabakh, a small enclave of historical Armenia cut off and enveloped within Azerbaijan by Stalin in the 1920s.

Ever since Nagorno-Karabakh was formed, the Azeri government has been trying to ethnically cleanse the Armenians from it. They have used cluster bombs, beheadings, rape, torture and pillage to carry out brutal deportations of entire villages. Baroness Cox first visited when war exploded in 1992. She brought back photographs of the atrocities, asked senior officials in the Foreign Office to provide support, and drew attention to Azerbaijan's war crimes in debates in the House of Lords. In 1993, she called for peace to be 'established and maintained' and for 'a political solution to be found'.[10]

She has been to the enclave more than ninety times since. In 2020, more than 91,000 people fled to Armenia from Nagorno-Karabakh. The invasion was deemed so severe that Genocide Watch issued a 'Genocide Emergency Alert'.[11] In the Queen's Speech debate in 2022, Baroness Cox said, 'I hope very much that the Government will no longer turn what seems to be a deaf ear to the suffering of the Armenian people in Nagorno-Karabakh.'

---

9   PD 23 February 1807 vol. 8 col. 977.
10 <https://api.parliament.uk/historic-hansard/lords/1993/oct/28/armenia-and-nagorno-karabakh> (accessed 13 July 2022).
11 <www.politicshome.com/thehouse/article/with-the-worlds-eyes-on-ukraine-azerbaijan-is-taking-full-advantage> and <https://hansard.parliament.uk/Lords/2022-01-06/debates/EE435C56-E534-4C1B-BD21-71E4CBFCF508/RefugeesMassDisplacement?highlight=nagorno#contribution-47606620-8FBA-4E94-9AA3-970F8B57D3B7> (both accessed 13 July 2022).

For decades, she has persevered, advocated, and told the stories of those persecuted worldwide. When asked what keeps her going, she says, 'The pain gives you the passion, and the passion gives you the energy.' The same was true of Wilberforce.

4 Community and companionship

Although Wilberforce is the person most easily remembered in connection with the anti-slavery movement, he surrounded himself with a network of exceptionally close evangelical friends united in the cause. The members of the Clapham Sect, as they came to be known years later, would talk for hours about politics and listen diligently to John Venn's gospel sermons.

William Wilberforce, Henry Thornton, James Stephen, Charles Grant, Edward Eliot and other Claphamites developed an affection, intimacy and openness usually found only among closest relatives.[12] Wilberforceans don't go it alone.

James Stephen ingeniously proposed the Bill which banned British ships from carrying slaves to French colonies. Revd Thomas Clarkson gathered compelling first-hand evidence of the slave trade. William Pitt said Wilberforce possessed the greatest natural eloquence of all the men he had ever known.[13] Wilberforce didn't find himself in the spotlight because he was the sole mover or chief visionary. It was his prowess in prose and public speaking, and his position in Parliament, that explains why he is remembered as the face of the campaign.

Each member of the Clapham Sect brought his or her own skills and experiences, and it was the value they all placed on harnessing their diverse traits that fuelled their success. As John Pollock eloquently explains, 'William Wilberforce is proof that a man can

---

12 Hague, *William Wilberforce*, p. 219.
13 John Piper, *Amazing Grace in the Life of William Wilberforce* (London: IVP, 2020), p. 29.

change his times, though he cannot do it alone.'[14] (Needless to say, this is true for women too!)

Throughout Hebrews 11, the list of people and their deeds of obedience and faith crescendos, culminating in Hebrews 12:1: 'Therefore, since we are surrounded by such a great cloud of witnesses, let us throw off everything that hinders and the sin that so easily entangles. And let us run with perseverance the race marked out for us.'

The language Paul uses is not 'Throw off' or 'You should throw off'; it's 'Let us throw off'. We are called to do good things in God's name in community with one another. If you have a goal in mind, talk about it. Surround yourself with people who can push you on, discern with you and pray for you. And do the same for others. Push them on. Discern with them. Pray with them. Ask them, 'What do you think God is saying to you?' 'How can I pray for you?' These are two of the best questions to ask. They take us to a deeper, more open level of Christian fellowship.

5 Declaration of faith

It's usually easier for us to refrain from explaining that our political principles are rooted in the character and teachings of Jesus. Either for fear of being sneered at, questioned about our views on this or that, or worry that the eternal salvation of our friend or colleague will then rest entirely on our shoulders, the temptation can be to hold back and tell half-truths about our world view. After all, as we have discussed, the quintessential British belief is that religion and politics shouldn't mix. Famously, Alastair Campbell, Director of Communications and Strategy for Prime Minister Tony Blair, abruptly interrupted one of Blair's interviews to point out, 'We don't do God.'

---

14 John Pollock, *A Man Who Changed His Times* (Burke, VA: Trinity Forum, 1996), p. 88.

But Wilberforce's Christian faith was not a hidden, underlying influence driving his pursuit for social justice; it was front and centre. He was as much about the advance of the gospel through his politics as he was about political pragmatism itself. It was impossible to hear one of his parliamentary interventions against the slave trade without knowing that it was God who had laid that injustice on his heart and God who had a far greater plan for humanity.

It's encouraging to hear Members of Parliament replicating Wilberforce's approach today. Many take the opportunity of their maiden speech – the first substantive speech following their election – to stand up and declare their faith. To take just one example, in 2019 Nick Fletcher became the Conservative MP for Don Valley, winning a seat which had been a part of Labour's 'red wall' for ninety-seven years. He used his maiden speech to state the following:

> I said in my acceptance speech that winning was nothing short of a miracle. I believe in miracles, and I believe in God . . . It is the reason I believe I am here – not to judge or condemn, but to listen, to help, to be kind, to forgive.[15]

From day one, Nick's cards were on the table. All of the MPs in the House of Commons Chamber at that moment – SNP, Conservative, Liberal Democrat or Labour – knew from then on that every just, humble and merciful contribution he made to debates, All-Party Parliamentary Groups and constituency surgeries was not that way just because he's a nice bloke, but because of something more.

For young Christians, the decision to advertise or abdicate their faith while at university is a challenge. So, imagine sitting in an opening Geography lecture at Newcastle University when, as a closing thought, Professor Nick Megoran says:

---

15 Hansard, HC, 16 March 2020, vol. 673, col. 692.

Every lecturer you encounter, every book you read, and every article you study at university comes from a certain perspective. Always ask yourself what the speaker or author's world views are, and how they influence what you have just read. For me, it's this: I am a follower of Jesus. I believe God made an extraordinarily wonderful world, and that our creator wants us to live in harmony with him, with each other and with the environment, and to secure justice between people.

Mic drop! For Professor Megoran, like Wilberforce, it's not just that his faith in Jesus drives his geopolitical work – he declares that it does. And once one deeply respected, unashamedly joyful professor has declared it with unbounded confidence in front of three hundred students, it makes it that much easier for the Christian students in that lecture theatre to say to their friends, 'Yes, I know that Jesus too.'

6 Repentance and redemption

William Wilberforce did not always live his life to such high standards. In 1776, he left his home town of Hull for the bright lights of St John's College, Cambridge University. And he blew it; he didn't work at his studies at all. Having inherited a large fortune from his father, Wilberforce was swept along by the culture of late-night drinking, playing cards, gambling and theatre-going, ultimately leaving with a degree without honours.[16] Later in life, he admitted that his behaviour at Cambridge and first years in Parliament were fuelled by the ambition of promoting his own career: 'My own distinction was my darling object.'[17] The point? Inspiring Christians aren't required to be perfect from cradle to grave.

---

16 Pollock, *A Man Who Changed His Times*, pp. 8–9; Hague, *William Wilberforce*, p. 23.
17 Pollock, p. 80.

Danielle Strickland certainly didn't have what many would consider a 'perfect' start in life. But she met Jesus in a jail cell, aged seventeen, and her aggressive compassion has served people in countries all over the world ever since.[18]

'I began to believe the lie of the Enemy – that rebellion is freedom – and went for it wholeheartedly,' Danielle says.[19] She was estranged from her family at thirteen years old, was in and out of prison for stealing cars and dealing drugs, and got kicked out of Christian campuses everywhere.[20] 'I thought that to give my life to Jesus meant that I had to clean it up first, and I was mistaken in that. You cannot clean up your life without Jesus.'[21]

Now, her life doesn't look anything like it once did. As she puts it in her book *A Beautiful Mess: How God re-creates our lives*: 'I've been re-created by a designer who loves to recycle.'[22] A large part of her adult life has been spent establishing church plants in inner-city areas that are impoverished, which led her into fighting against sexual exploitation of women and boys. She has founded and leads a multitude of global justice and advocacy movements and launched global anti-trafficking initiatives, including Brave Global, Amplify Peace, and 'imby'. Danielle also co-founded Stop The Traffik, a campaign coalition founded to bring an end to human trafficking worldwide, which successfully lobbied Cadbury's to make a commitment that Dairy Milk would become Fairtrade in the UK.[23]

If you've understood the characteristics of a Wilberforcean but discount yourself, or someone else, from pursuing a life of political purpose because you think you've made too many mistakes for God to use you, then you may as well stop reading! In Philippians 1, Paul

18 <www.youtube.com/watch?v=FsurLU4njlY> (accessed 13 July 2022).
19 <www.youtube.com/watch?v=BwuWWXgLcuw&t=3s> (accessed 13 July 2022).
20 <www.youtube.com/watch?v=x7NKMEgjwpM> (accessed 13 July 2022).
21 <www.youtube.com/watch?v=FsurLU4njlY> (accessed 13 July 2022).
22 Danielle Strickland, *A Beautiful Mess: How God re-creates our lives* (Oxford: Monarch, 2014), p. 11.
23 <www.christiantoday.com/article/stop.the.traffik.welcomes.cadburys.switch.to.fairtrade/22696.htm> (accessed 14 July 2022).

and Timothy write, 'I always pray with joy . . . being confident of this, that he who began a good work in you will carry it on to completion until the day of Christ Jesus' (vv. 4, 6).

God will redeem all of those fragments of your broken past and put them together as a tapestry of his grace. As Catherine Campbell states in the title of her book about people God used mightily, 'God isn't finished with you yet'.[24]

Conclusion

As God did with Wilberforce, he will use some of us as MPs. But many of us will be called elsewhere, and we can still be politically engaged in those places. If we pursue the character and manner of Wilberforce, we will see significant changes that cast out injustice wherever we are.

To recap how to be a Wilberforcean:

1 Refine your focus.
2 Use what God has put in your hands.
3 Move on with perseverance and determination.
4 Immerse yourself in community.
5 Be honest about your faith.
6 Remember that you aren't too broken.

We shouldn't dilute what it means to be like Wilberforce: it is terrifically hard, enduring work. But hopefully this chapter has made the task seem more digestible.

So, Wilberforce provides a model for Christian engagement in politics, but how do we put it into practice? The next section has some suggestions for exploring some of the next steps you might want to take.

---

24 Catherine Campbell, *God Isn't Finished With You Yet* (London: IVP, 2022).

Case study: Mabon ap Gwynfor, Member of the Senedd (MS)

Three threads from Mabon ap Gwynfor's family background have run through his life and career in politics: Welsh nationalism, peace activism and Christianity.

Mabon is the grandson of the first Plaid Cymru MP, Gwynfor Evans. He has 'vivid memories' of campaigning with his grandfather from the age of four, holding his hand while drumming up votes in Carmarthen. This family background 'instilled in me that we have a duty to stand up for others, people we don't know. To do something for our brothers and sisters wherever they are.' He recognized that politics was a way in which he 'could become a voice for somebody else'. That idea runs through many of the case studies in this book – to follow the biblical command to be a voice for the voiceless. Far from a cliché, it is a common motivation to defend the trampled in whatever way we can.

Furthermore, Mabon's parents were peace activists on various campaigns and peace marches. The 9/11 terror attacks and subsequent war in Iraq 'struck a chord in me that there's something really wrong here. We can't resolve differences by killing each other.'

With this family background it was, possibly, inevitable that Mabon would at least take an interest in politics. Faith in Jesus, however, had to come independently. He grew up in church and faith, but it was during a group trip to Lindisfarne Monastery as a teenager that he had an 'awakening' to the reality of Jesus Christ as his Saviour.

He has since campaigned and won a seat in the Welsh Senedd. The last couple of months of the election campaign, and the first few months as an MS, were a trial. Mabon 'struggled' with his mental health throughout this time. It was a combination of causes. 'The pressure of expectations, because of my family connections, because of my Christianity. Knowing, because I've been so involved in politics, that you have to compromise in politics and compromise isn't easy ... I like to believe I'm a man of principles ... and knowing that I might have to compromise those principles was really weighing heavily on my mind. How do I reconcile my faith, my upbringing, my principles, with some of the things that I might have to do in my post? I've come to terms with it now and it's a case of learning day by day.'

Making faith public, as Mabon has experienced, is not an easy choice to make – our lives and careers might well be made easier if faith was kept privately tucked away. But that is not what we are called to. When it comes to compromise, Mabon is still figuring out, 'day by day', where the line between acceptable and unacceptable compromise lies. After all, compromising politics might be necessary practically, whereas compromising theology might be a step too far. Regardless, Christians have the peace that comes with humility, knowing we are not perfect, and knowing we cannot change the world entirely by our own efforts. This peace helps us as we seek to work and to serve others and live out our faith publicly, all for the glory of God.

Part 3

HOW CHRISTIANS COULD ENGAGE WITH POLITICS

10

By paying attention and praying

When I'm in church and the worship leader moves on to praying for our government, I confess to feeling a bit awkward. Will she mention me, as the local MP? What sort of posture do I adopt if she does – nodding along gratefully, or maintaining a kind of static embarrassment?

Like many Christians, I don't pray enough. When I do pray, I usually spend at least part of my confessional time repenting for not praying. Like all sins, omission of prayer is not just disobedient; it is stupid too. Why? Because prayer is our opportunity to go directly to the Creator of the universe, the one who holds all things in his hands, who is intimately concerned about every aspect of our lives.

Hebrews 4:16 says, 'Let us then approach God's throne of grace with confidence, so that we may receive mercy and find grace to help us in our time of need.' Here is a picture of us being invited to approach the King's throne, which because of God's grace, we now have open permission to do.

I'm never quite sure whether, as a Christian, I am meant to like the 1990s comedy series *Father Ted*. Truth is, though, I absolutely love it. There are so many ridiculous scenarios and classic lines. On one occasion, Ted turns to his assistant priest Dougal and whispers to him nervously about an elderly parishioner who he suspects knows more than he wants her to. He suggests that old women are closer to God than priests can ever be. They no longer need the operator to connect them to God, because they've been given a direct line. The thing is, though, if you trust Jesus as your Saviour, you don't need an operator either. The direct line is always open.[1]

There are lots of reasons why we don't pick up the phone. Sometimes it might be that we don't know what to say. When it comes to praying about politics, I think that is especially so.

But in Philippians 4:6 we are told, 'Do not be anxious about anything, but in every situation, by prayer and petition, with thanksgiving, present your requests to God.' There is a whole sermon to be given on that one verse, so let's pick up on just one thing: 'in every situation' – which means that there is no aspect of life we aren't to pray about.

Politics is the business of how we order and run our society – there are few things more 'everything' than that!

So, of course we should pray about politics and politicians. Yet because many Christians see politics as such a mucky business, they hide away from it. Or else they see politicians as so untrustworthy that they pay scant attention to what they think and say. The end result is that Christians often have too little information (and maybe too little inclination) to even know where to start when it comes to praying about politics.

Let's look at it this way. If a friend at church tells you that his mother is ill, you will most likely offer to pray for her – and it would be normal in those circumstances to ask your friend what his mother's name is and what her condition is. You can then lift her up to God in prayer by name and ask for his intervention in her illness.

It's the same with politics. It makes sense that we should want to know enough to pray in an informed way about the issues and the people involved.

So how might we approach praying about politics?

---

1 Note for youngsters: once upon a time in the ancient past, when you made a phone call, you'd first get through to an operator who would then connect you to the person you wanted to speak to – and yes, you had to literally dial the number in the first place, using an actual dial. Happy times, just a bit more complicated . . .

Pay attention

Politics matters to God because people matter to him. And if politics matters, then we should dedicate at least a little time to understanding political events. Lots of us avoid watching the news, understandably perhaps, given that so much of it seems either miserable or trivial. But if we want to be informed in our prayer and in our concern then we need to watch, listen to and read the news – and be careful to do so from a balanced perspective.

Choose your platform wisely. In the UK, much of our media has an express bias. We simply need to be aware of that before exposing ourselves to it – so that we can take what we learn with the appropriate 'pinch of salt'. A quick summary: Channel 4 will be a bit liberal or left wing; most of the print media will be significantly right wing (apart from *The Guardian*, *The Mirror*, *The i* and, to an extent, the *Financial Times*); the BBC and ITV News will be fairly neutral. I find that the BBC tends to be attacked for being full of lefty liberals by the right-wingers, and for being full of establishment conservatives by the lefty liberals – which means that it is probably in just about the right place! Of course, all news providers are biased to some extent, but some are consciously, deliberately biased whereas others – such as the BBC – are only biased in the sense that they imbibe and then regurgitate the culture of the age. Mostly, however, the broadcast media in the UK will consciously attempt to be 'above' politics and tell the news from a non-partisan position. Personally, I think we in the UK are enormously fortunate in this respect.

What should we believe?

The term 'fake news' has become part of our twenty-first-century vocabulary, and not without justification. The rise and expansion of the internet opens us up to information from an almost infinite number of sources. According to Bernard Marr in an article written for *Forbes* in May 2018, 90% of the data in the world at that stage had been created in the previous two years![2] So, from 2016 to 2018, there was nine times more information produced (and shared) than from the birth of civilization up to 2015. This is mind-blowing. There is so much more news and information out there than there was a generation ago. Most of it will not be verified, well researched or referenced, much of it will be – to coin a phrase – absolute garbage . . . yet to many people it may have the same standing as an article on the BBC website or a peer-reviewed piece in an academic journal.

As Christians, we should be committed to telling the truth. That means we have a specific calling to understand the extent to which something is true, an opinion based on credible facts, an opinion based on non-credible 'facts' or just a total lie. We should not be sharing as truth something that is not true or something that we do not know to be true. In Matthew 10:16 Jesus sends out his disciples into the world, warning them to be as 'shrewd as snakes and as innocent as doves'. We should be gracious towards those who hold different opinions, but not gullible or credulous – and we certainly must not be accomplices in spreading things that are not true, simply because they conform to what we already think. When we pray, we should pray on the basis of things that are true, which means that we should be careful.

I would also suggest that – even if you only gain your information from credible, non-biased sources – you will be missing out if you don't look to sources of news in your own community.

The American politician Tip O'Neill once said, 'All politics is local.' As well as keeping on top of national and international issues, it makes sense to engage in the politics of the place where you live. If you want to understand the issues of your local community you could become one of the dwindling band (like me) who read a local newspaper. Listen to the local radio station, follow local online groups, even read

---

2 <www.forbes.com/sites/bernardmarr/2018/05/21/how-much-data-do-we-create-every-day-the-mind-blowing-stats-everyone-should-read> (accessed 13 July 2022).

the leaflets delivered by your local councillors or prospective councillors (they will of course be biased – but at least openly so!).

Is your church involved in social action through a food bank, a debt advice centre, a housing need charity? Through those movements you can find out about the issues that are most relevant to the local community. You can also see the impact of national government policies on real families.

With all this in mind, you should keep an eye on the news and pray that some events and people will stand out to you, move your heart and leave you wanting things to change. Something will stand out to you for sure, whether it be the experience of families living in poverty, people struggling with mental health conditions, the state of cancer services, integrity among our politicians, freedom of religious belief, our treatment of those seeking asylum, a local planning decision or crime in the local area.

Commit to praying for these issues, and to informing yourself about them and the people involved.

Pray for yourself

One of the things that God promises to give us if we ask for it is wisdom. As we commit to praying for our politicians and for current affairs, let's first ask God for wisdom for ourselves. Proverbs 1:20 (ESV) tells us that 'wisdom cries aloud in the street' (NIV: 'raises her voice in the public square'), indicating that wisdom is not hidden away – it is freely available. James says, 'If any of you lacks wisdom, you should ask God, who gives generously to all without finding fault, and it will be given to you' (James 1:5).

I have heard it said that 'wisdom is a plenteous crop with a meagre harvest'! Wisdom is freely available to all, but too few avail themselves of it because too few ask. Let us be those who ask.

Ask for wisdom to discern the true from the untrue, to understand the issues and to weigh them up fairly, and for a heart of compassion. In all things it is important to pray that we would remain humble before God, knowing that, however wise we may get, we will never know everything – and that it is always possible an opinion formed in good faith might turn out to be wrong. Pray that we would see issues and see people as God sees them – in which case, no person's troubles will be trivial to us. At the same time, let us understand that politics – important though it is – is not the route to ultimately solving the world's problems. It is right to pray to have a passion for serving people and meeting their needs through politics, while at the same time praying that politics does not become an ultimate thing in which we place our faith.

Do not become overwhelmed. You cannot solve all the world's problems. You cannot even solve all the problems of your own community. I am a Member of Parliament and so politics is my full-time job, and yet I have to prioritize and choose to focus on issues where I think I can make a difference. I would say that five issues take up the majority of my time: radiotherapy cancer treatment, farming, affordable housing in the Lake District, refugees and mental health provision. If I don't specialize at least a bit, then I simply won't be effective and I could easily be even more overwhelmed than I already am!

What to pray for

You will be more effective in your work and more informed in your prayers if you choose to focus.

Twenty-four-hour news, constant social media, the never-ending torrent of information we are now subject to . . . all this brings with it a number of disadvantages. Two of these are 'compassion fatigue' and 'outrage fatigue'.

The plight of hungry young children in Afghanistan, forced to go out to work to feed themselves and their families, featured much in the British media over the Christmas period in 2021. Within days, the front pages moved on to some other tragedy somewhere else. Some people will have found an appropriate charity to donate to in order to help those children, some will have prayed, but most will have felt sad briefly before moving on, their capacity for compassion depleted, their attention diverted. Yet those children remain in their dreadful circumstances and are of immense value to God.

Meanwhile, it turned out that a certain UK politician who had ordained that people could not see their loved ones at Christmas 2020, due to Covid, had in fact himself been having parties with friends at the time. One rule for us, no rules for them, so to speak. People were outraged . . . for a while.

Further afield, we see the detention of Hong Kong human rights protesters by the Chinese government, war crimes committed by Russian soldiers against Ukrainian civilians, and the actions of powerful people involved in sex trafficking of children and young people. The right response to these outrages is to be outraged. But when the news cycle moves on to something else and then something else after that, our capacity to be angry and demand justice can wane under the volume of information and the pressures of life.

As an aside, I strongly suspect that some in authority use 'outrage fatigue' as a tactic. In other words, they do something terrible, then sit tight and soak up the outrage from press and public for a few days before seeing that outrage dissipate. After which, the pressure on them to apologize, resign or change course evaporates.

As Christians, we must not get compassion or outrage fatigue. I want to encourage you to find an issue, or issues, that you are passionate about, and to 'always pray and not give up' (Luke 18:1).

Who to pray for

Politicians come in all shapes and sizes! Knowing who our politicians are and what they do is an important first step when it comes to praying for them! For instance, when we are praying for the right action to be taken on Covid or on cancer treatment, then it would make sense to know who the Secretary of State for Health is, and who his or her opposite number is, and then to learn about their priorities and background so that we might pray for them in an informed way.

As you will see from appendix B, which illustrates 'who's who' across the political world, politics is about people – and it is full of people. Not just the people you serve if you are elected but also the people who are part of your team. Caring for them and motivating them is as important a part of my role as anything else. Our democracy cannot function without them and we should be grateful to them and for them, whatever the colour of their rosette!

There are a lot of people to pray for!

What should we consider when we pray?

Remember that politicians are human beings too! God loves politicians, which means that we should too. In addition, the well-being of a politician can have a huge impact on the decisions that he or she makes.

As a student at Newcastle University, the most enjoyable course that I took was 'Psychology of Politics', which was led by the late great Professor Hugh Berrington. There were around thirty people registered on the course, but the attendance at the lectures would often exceed a hundred – such was their entertainment value.

Hugh reduced the policy outcomes of the administrations of Winston Churchill, Lyndon Johnson, Richard Nixon and Anthony Eden to the psychological issues within each of these men. He was particularly acerbic about Nixon. In 1990, when I did this course, Richard Nixon had been out of office for seventeen years, yet Professor Berrington remained active as the Treasurer of the British Anti-Nixon Society. This passion would reveal itself during lectures as the great professor would go on one venomous diversion after another.

The case study that really grabbed my attention was the contention – backed up by an article in 2003 by Lord David Owen in *QJM*, the international journal of medicine – that the Suez Crisis of 1956 owed much to the state of health of the then Prime Minister, Sir Anthony Eden. In particular, the impact on his outlook caused by operations on his gallbladder. Both Professor Berrington and Lord Owen suggest that Eden's physical and subsequent mental health left him feeling personally affronted and humiliated by the actions of Egyptian president Abdel Nasser surrounding access to the Suez Canal. Eden is reported to have become short-tempered, thin-skinned and incapable of making wise decisions, leading eventually to the failed Franco-British military attempt to seize control of the canal.[3]

I won't go into the details here, but it is fair to say that the Suez Crisis counts as the great British foreign policy disaster of the second half of the twentieth century. The humiliating climbdown that Eden had to make under US pressure effectively confirmed the UK's relegation from its status as a first-class world power.

If only people had been praying for Eden's gallbladder . . . or at least for wisdom and patience in Eden's decision-making!

My point, when I say that politicians are people too, is that not only should we have loving compassion for them but we should also be aware that their decisions will be affected by how they are physically, mentally, emotionally and spiritually. When we pray for our politicians, we must be mindful that they are complex human beings who will not always find it easy to compartmentalize their political lives and their private lives. If we want to pray for good and

---

3 David Owen, the Rt Hon Lord, 'Diseased, demented, depressed: serious illness in Heads of State', *QJM: An International Journal of Medicine*, vol. 96, no. 5 (May 2003), pp. 325–336: <https://doi.org/10.1093/qjmed/hcg061>. Peter Hennessy's biography *The Prime Minister: The office and its holders since 1945* quotes Churchill's doctor, Lord Moran, as recorded in Harold Macmillan's diary, confiding that he 'thought Eden would have great difficulty standing the strain [of the premiership]. The state of his inside is not good, and he ought to be careful' (London: Penguin, 2000, p. 209).

wise decisions, we should be mindful of the well-being of the decision-makers.

The state of politicians' relationships matters too. Getting elected to Parliament in the early hours of Friday 6 May 2005 was a huge achievement for me – and for my family. But I remember our tears on the Sunday night as we prepared for me to travel down to Westminster for the first time the following morning. So began seventeen years (and counting) of me spending two or three nights a week away from my wife and our children. I would urge us all to pray for politicians and for their families, for time together, for wise parenting, for marital faithfulness. In addition, let's remember that MPs have constituencies that they serve and where – mostly – they live, while at the same time being focused on the business of government and of Parliament. It is so important for MPs to get the balance right between duties of national governance and legislation, and their primary duty to serve the community that elected them.

Earlier, we considered the need to pray for wisdom for ourselves. We should also pray for wisdom for our leaders. We could do a lot worse than consider the prayer used at the beginning of business in the UK's House of Commons each day:

> Lord, the God of righteousness and truth, grant to our Queen and her government, to Members of Parliament and all in positions of responsibility, the guidance of your Spirit. May they never lead the nation wrongly through love of power, desire to please, or unworthy ideals but laying aside all private interests and prejudices keep in mind their responsibility to seek to improve the condition of all mankind; so may your kingdom come and your name be hallowed.[4]

---

4 <www.parliament.uk/about/how/business/prayers> (accessed 11 July 2022).

Attending prayers at the beginning of the parliamentary day is for many effectively just the opportunity to bag your seat for that day – the parliamentary equivalent of the Germans putting their beach towels on the sun loungers. Nevertheless, this is a good prayer!

Often we do not know what we should ask for. Should we ask for the coronavirus to disappear? Should we ask for restrictions to stop the spread of the disease, for greater freedoms, or for prioritization of cancer and mental health services, for financial support for affected businesses? How do we pray about the war in Ukraine and the actions of the UK government and other Western countries in trying to stop Putin? We can be sure that God knows what should be done, and so we should ask him to guide our leaders into wise decisions, and pray that those who give advice would be wise too. Politicians can hear much advice, a lot of it conflicting; the art of government is to choose who and what to listen to – that is where wisdom is most needed.

The parliamentary prayer reminds us that integrity is vital too. It can be so tempting to go with the flow, to follow public opinion, to see what the polls say and then simply do that. Wise and decent leadership will, however, sometimes involve actual leadership! In other words, sometimes a leader will have to take a decision which is right but unpopular, and then persuade the people to follow.

Politicians are inveterate people-pleasers – not just because we need votes to be elected but also because there is something of the performer in many of us. Maybe one of the reasons some people are drawn into politics is that they have a need to be loved, even adored. Professor Berrington would claim that the late President Reagan was one such example. Is that all bad?

'Democrats should follow the will of the people,' I hear you say. Yes, but sometimes they should lead the people, challenge them and point towards a wiser path, and then accept defeat if they cannot succeed in persuading them.

Praying for integrity among our politicians – individually and collectively – ought to be at the top of our lists. There are three particular temptations that I think politicians are prone to, and that I know we would appreciate your prayers for:

- the temptation to make decisions that benefit the powerful or the vocal;
- the temptation to pursue ideological purity at a cost to the welfare of the people;
- the temptation to feather one's own nest, to act in ways that bring personal or even financial advantage.

All have sinned and fall short of the glory of God. That includes each of us, and it includes everyone in politics.

For the tens of thousands of councillors and volunteers involved in our political system, our prayers should also be for them to get the balance right between their work and family lives on the one hand and their political service on the other.

I would say this, wouldn't I? But people in politics expose themselves to loss and rejection, to vilification and sometimes even violence. Those who do it voluntarily are especially in need of our support and prayers. But for all who make themselves vulnerable in this way, let us pray for them to be strengthened and resilient, to be gracious under fire, and let us also be thankful for them.

An important part of our Christian witness is how we relate to politicians. Be mindful then of the impact you have on them – and on their staff and volunteers – as a result of whatever you write or say to them or about them. Why not reach out to your councillor, your MP, MSP, MS, MLA or a locally based peer, and make common cause with him or her on an issue that you both care about? In doing so, you can ask these individuals if you can pray for them – and then do pray for them, regularly and passionately. Plead with God that there might be progress on the issue at hand, and plead with

God that they might come to know Jesus as Lord and Saviour for themselves.

Christians in politics

There are dozens of Christian MPs and lords in Westminster and thousands of Christians involved in the wider politics of the UK. All that I have said above completely applies to those of us in politics who are believers. In addition, though, I have found that we need prayer when it comes to the quality of our walk with God.

Possibly my biggest error as a Christian in Parliament has been in regard to fellowship – or lack of it – with brothers and sisters in Christ. My family and I regularly attend our local church on Sunday, but I am normally down in London until Wednesday or Thursday night and so I rarely get to our house group, or fix informal time with friends at church to pray regularly. In my first term as an MP I was involved in Bible study and fellowship with Christian MPs, but once I was elected as Party President in 2010 and then Leader in 2015, I allowed all those increasing time pressures to squeeze out time for fellowship. The people around me – who were great people – were mostly not Christians and therefore, understandably, didn't quite see the value in protecting diary time for me to meet with other believers – and so, through my own lack of discipline, I became somewhat isolated. I am sure that I would have made wiser choices and been a far better MP and, more importantly, a far more useful witness for Christ if I had exerted that discipline over myself by building and protecting fellowship with other believers. Since I stepped down as Leader, things have improved considerably in that regard.

My experience is one that leads me to encourage you to pray for Christians in politics that they would not give up meeting with one another and that they would have brothers and sisters who support them, hold them accountable, and help them to grow in discipleship and understanding. If you have an MP or a councillor, or someone who works in politics in some other role, who is a Christian, why not offer to lead a prayer group for him or her?

Christians especially need prayer for them to remain faithful to the Lord, not to slip into easy policy positions that reflect the current culture but are opposed to what the Bible teaches. At the same time, we need wisdom and courage not to unthinkingly take a particular position just because it is held by an influential Christian with whom we would normally agree. Pray for us not to get swept up in culture wars, from either side, but to be humbly faithful to Christ.

As a Christian in politics, I have found that I am able to use what limited profile I have to speak openly about the gospel to audiences – virtual and physical – that might not otherwise hear it. This is a huge blessing, and a huge responsibility for which most of us are not really trained. Please pray that we would use the opportunities that we have to tell people about Jesus in ways that draw people to him as their Lord and Saviour and bring glory to him. If we are known as Christians, we are going to get asked tough questions about the many countercultural things that the Bible teaches us, so we need prayer to give answers that are wise, truthful and gentle. Without going over old wounds, it's true that my time in politics could have been quite different if I had been less complacent about these things!

I have seen people come to commit their lives to Jesus during their time in Parliament, but I have also seen people fall away from their faith. I cannot see into a person's heart, but it seems to me that the main drivers that push a Christian in politics to backslide, and even to deny Christ, are the pressure to conform to the culture in general, the pressure to conform for career reasons and, sadly, sexual unfaithfulness. Please pray for all involved in politics that they may be kept safe.

For me, the temptation to conform was huge. Christians are not legalists. We are saved by grace. Let's not hold politicians up to a standard that none of us can ever reach. Maybe the most powerful and transformational experience of my Christian life was the moment when, after I had denied the truth in order to conform one time, a brother told me, 'For the Christian, sin spoils our relationship with God . . . but it doesn't end it. It doesn't end it.' That blew me away and brought me to my knees. Pray that Christians involved in politics would believe for themselves and share with others that they are sinners saved by grace. The expectations of perfection and upstanding-ness among our politicians can lead us to behave like legalists even if we say that we are not. Our entry into God's family is by grace alone, and our continuing in his eternal loving care is also by grace alone, not by our achievements. We need to remember that for ourselves and for all those for whom we pray.

Praying even for *them?*

In the course of recording three series of the Mucky Business podcast, I note that of the fifty or so people I have interviewed so far as guests on the show, only three of them belong to the same political party as me. I have interviewed Christians who think the opposite to me on Brexit, the opposite to me on Scottish independence, the opposite to me on certain Covid issues and the opposite to me – of course – on whether or not we should have a Conservative government!

I have enjoyed hearing the differing perspectives held by Christians from across the political spectrum. It has been a privilege to pray for people who are my political opponents, yet who are also my brothers and sisters in Christ.

A term that Christians in the world of politics often use to describe what we need to do is: 'disagree well'. I think this is a really important part of our witness. We can seek to understand the other person's perspective, and be gracious towards him or her personally, while holding a very different point of view ourselves.

129

If you are a Christian who disagrees strongly with the government of the day, or who is opposed to the views of your local MP or councillor, I still think you should pray for that individual. When it comes to your local representatives, it's right to seek to meet them so they know that while you may disagree with them, you value them and you pray for them.

'Disagreeing well' is not the same thing as agreeing with someone. It's far tougher! Yet, the same grace we receive from God, we are asked to show towards others. Behaving graciously towards someone we disagree with does not, however, mean that we need to become soppily neutral. Too often, I fear that Christians are expected to hold positions akin to the worst caricature of the usually anodyne 'Thought for the Day' slot on Radio 4's *Today* programme – a slot I consider to be offensively inoffensive. In being called to be gentle, humble and gracious, I don't think we are called to sit on the fence when it comes to matters that are simply wrong. In our prayers, let us sincerely hold before the Lord politicians of every rank and every variety, let us hold up those affected by decisions large and small, and let us not hold back. We must pray as if it matters. Because it does.

When we see the carnage in Afghanistan and Ukraine, the lives lived in despair in so many communities in the UK, the impact of changes in the climate on millions of people across the globe, our prayers should surely take the form of the laments that we read in the Psalms and the book of Lamentations. Let's bang on God's door in pleading distress. When we pray, we pray to the sovereign God who promises to listen and whose will is perfect. Our words will not fall on deaf ears. When it comes to politics and politicians, we should approach God with humility, yet also with courage.

Case study: Derek Thomas MP

When Derek Thomas, MP for St Ives in Cornwall, the son of missionary parents, found out that the G7 summit was being held in his constituency, there was a quick and firm reaction. To pray.

Derek and a group of other Cornish Christian leaders met every Friday morning to pray for an hour. This former businessman is a practical person, a campaigning local MP, vocal about bread-and-butter local issues such as farming, the environment and housing. His first and continuous action was to pray because prayer is a tool that works.

He and his friends 'prayed ... a lot'. Pragmatic prayers – that the summit would go well and smoothly, for the safety and security of all involved. Significantly, they prayed for the world leaders gathering there. For wisdom, for humility, for good decisions to be made.

A significant issue was the climate crisis. They prayed that this group of some of the most powerful people on earth would have humility in approaching a huge impersonal challenge such as climate change. 'We really wanted them to recognize that it's God who provides all that we have, God who creates all that we enjoy,' and while we have responsibilities for the planet, 'we are not actually top of the tree'. They prayed that the leaders would view the environment not as a resource to endlessly plunder, but as an amazing gift to steward responsibly. That they would have the wisdom to see the gravity of the situation. That they would have the decisiveness to act urgently.

Every prayer 'was always conscious of God's heart for the poor'. The leaders present represented only 60% of the world's population. The poorest 40% were not given a voice. The group prayed earnestly that the summit would find a way to recover from the pandemic that would not crush other countries in the process.

Prayers about climate change must often be vague and sprawling, since the problem is bigger and more threatening than we can comprehend. Sometimes we must lament, and sometimes we must pray with anger at what humanity has done to creation. The members of the group were informed about the issues; they understood the challenges the summit would face. They were informed, so their prayers were informed.

Their immediate prayers were answered – the event went well, with no safety concerns, and there were environmental targets agreed. The future significance remains to be seen in the years ahead as the looming threat of climate disaster approaches.

Whatever the ensuing outcome of the G7 summit, the group set an example of how we should all engage with politics – especially when it seems as though we can't have any influence at all, shut off behind security barriers while leaders swan about for summits and photo shoots. That example is prayer. Prayer that is informed, earnest, continuous, specific, vague, small – and huge.

11

By being the one who shows up

By this point in the book you may be excited and raring to go, or maybe you're overwhelmed and still a bit uncertain. Either way, the question remains: where do you begin? We have told you that being involved in politics is important ... but what now? There will undoubtedly be a spectrum of knowledge and understanding of the mechanics of politics among those reading this book. If you are one of the people who would previously have said, 'I don't keep up with politics,' or if you have preferred to bury your head in the sand, it may feel as though you need several years of study and a library's worth of books to consider yourself 'informed'. When the conversation turns to politics, it can seem as if everyone has started speaking a foreign language and you can't make head nor tail of it. But don't worry, we are not here to give you an extensive reading list.

Let's split the small steps you can take into two broad categories: your politics and your politicians.

Engaging in your community

First, your politics. As we have established, politics touches all our lives whether we like it or not. So when we speak about 'your politics', we are talking about the politics you can engage in yourself; the places you can get your hands dirty; the things that are going on in your local community that you can personally get involved with.

There are many ways to get our hands dirty for God. We may be called to set up a charity to deliver food parcels to the needy, or to drive a delivery van, or to give money to the charities that do so, or to pray for them.

We may find our passion in any number of places. As Paul reminds us in Romans 12 and 1 Corinthians 12, though we are many, we are one body in Christ, and we are all given different gifts and different roles to play.

The main thing, as we have seen, is that when we seek to put Jesus first and to serve and obey him in love, we find that he gives us an increasing love for others and a desire to serve them in practical ways. One springs from the other. In the words of the 1990s band DC Talk, 'Luv Is a Verb'. Or as James put it in his letter, 'Faith without deeds is useless' (James 2:20).

So, what is your passion and your heartbreak? What impels you to get stuck in and get your hands dirty? And what might this look like?

It is easy to be daunted by the mess of the world around us and not know where to start. So here are some tips.

As Christians, of course, and as we set out in the previous chapter, the first, continual and last thing we should do is to pray. If God has put something on your heart, he will have an idea about what he would like you to do with it. Maybe you could join in with the worship song mentioned earlier, asking God to break your heart for what breaks his, and empower you to give your whole self for his kingdom.

And prayer may be the key thing that God is asking you to do. Even as Christians, we generally underestimate the power and importance of prayer. When we feel helpless in the face of a situation, how many of us have thought, *All I can do is pray*? But prayer is never a poor substitute. It is the power of God in every situation. Prayer support for existing ventures is vital, and perhaps God wants you to pray for others to be raised up.

Writer and speaker Jennifer Rees-Larcombe told a story about an old woman who lived by herself and never went out into her community. But on her dining-room table she had a dog-eared map of her local town, and every day she would walk her finger down a different street and pray for the people living there. This was a faithful outworking of God's command in Jeremiah 29:7 (ESV) to 'seek the welfare of the city where I have sent you', and an inspiring example of what it means to 'pray without ceasing' (1 Thessalonians 5:17). It was done quietly and without fanfare, without even leaving the house, but this woman was getting her hands dirty in God's service.

Once you have started praying, look around you.

Identifying what to get involved in should be a combination of what we are passionate about and where the need is. We are unlikely to maintain a sustained interest and investment in something that we aren't passionate about. But equally, we need to be conscious of the needs of our community, not just looking for our own hobby horse.

There are a few ways to go about this that will vary depending on your capacity and the time you are able to dedicate. It is a wise precaution to know your capacity and to set boundaries around the time, energy and resources you are able to give. For the particularly empathetic and passionate, the need in front of you may feel overwhelming and you can become tempted to overstretch yourself. But make sure you temper this with what is realistic and sustainable. It's OK to start small, for example by spending an hour every fortnight volunteering at a local charity, and you can always increase that.

Equally, you may feel as though you have no capacity at all. After so many months of pandemic, a lot of people are feeling overwhelmed by the sheer weight of living life. God knows and cares about our situation. But we should also try to keep our hearts open to his gentle promptings. And it is frequently true that we are able to make time for the things we really care about. An hour a week is not a lot, but you may need to think strategically about how you fit it in and sacrifice some time being spent elsewhere.

Once you have thought about your capacity, you need to start listening. Open your eyes and your ears to the people and places around you. Where has God placed you? Where do you interact with your community – in your local neighbourhood, the park, a nearby café, a church, your children's school or afterschool clubs, an old people's home, your workplace, your college or apprenticeship, the corner shop, well-known footpaths and green spaces, on public transport, in the doctor's surgery? These are all places in our community, places where we live, work and play.

Wherever God has placed you, you can be his hands and feet in your community. You may feel that what you do is unimportant. But remember that God told Zechariah not to despise the day of small things. In 1 Corinthians 1:27, Paul tells us that 'God chose the foolish things of the world to shame the wise; God chose the weak things of the world to shame the strong'. This is so that we can boast not in our own strength and wisdom, but in his.

In the Bible, God used all kinds of people just where they were. When talking of political involvement, we often refer to Joseph, Daniel, Esther and Nehemiah, who all held important and responsible roles in their communities.

But God also used the Shunammite woman who took in Elisha, gave him a room in her house and cared for him whenever he was in the region (2 Kings 4); Rahab who hid the Israelite spies in Jericho (Joshua 2); Dorcas who 'was always doing good and helping the poor' in Joppa (Acts 9:36); and Lydia, a dealer in cloth, who invited Paul and his friends to stay with her in Thyatira (Acts 16:15). These people have quite small roles in the Bible, but God chose to work through them in their communities, right where they were.

We don't need to do everything with a loud fanfare. As has been said earlier, as far as we know, Daniel served quietly in Babylon for years before the lions' den episode.

It may be that you are already conscious of the injustices and needs you see around you. But often we are so busy getting on with life that we don't even really take notice, or at least not beyond their direct impact on us. Sometimes we can find it very easy to proselytize an idea and complain, but it never really gets much further. Here are a few steps you can take to begin to change this.

1 Consider what you find yourself complaining about most often. Is the traffic around the school entrance dangerous for the kids? Is the park in disrepair? Is it the litter in your community that concerns you, or the lack of cycle routes to your workplace? Is it antisocial behaviour?

2 Consciously walk around with your eyes open. If you can't think of any problems, spend a week or two – maybe even a month – consciously praying for, thinking about and engaging with the people and needs you see around you.

3 Spend some time looking into a particular issue. What lies behind it? For example, if the problem is antisocial behaviour, part of the reason may be that there are no youth services in your community.

4 Contact your local councillor. As well as using your own eyes and ears, it is also worth dropping an email to your local councillor and asking him or her where the needs are in your neighbourhood. The results of this may vary, but if you're in any luck, your councillor will be incredibly grateful to hear from you and be able to provide helpful insights into what is going on behind the scenes in your area. This is also a great way to establish a supportive relationship with those politicians serving your community.

5 Search online to discover what is already going on. When it comes to finding out which charities are operating locally or which projects are taking place, a search engine is your friend. The chances are that if you have noticed an issue, others will have too.

You don't need to start something new, or to act alone. There will undoubtedly be many services already being delivered quietly in your community. Most of them will be run by a core handful of people, who will generally welcome new volunteers to help share the load. This could be the local scout group, a toddler group, the Citizens Advice Bureau. If you are moved by the rising poverty at this time, you may feel called to donate to your local food bank, to encourage your church or school or local supermarket to collect items on its behalf, or to go and help out with sorting and delivering the donations. The church is called to be relational in the local neighbourhood: we are not a lot of fragmented individuals all doing our thing but rather a community of believers. We can work together and support one another at the same time.

6 Pick an issue and decide on your next steps. Narrow down what you come up with to something that you want to invest in – and go for it! You may want to get in touch with the relevant charity, or your email to your councillor may have already got the ball rolling. Whatever it might be, take that next step.

We won't promise that engaging in local politics will not involve any work – because it will. But so it should. We are making the case that this is important. It is important for Christians to be involved in loving and caring for their communities. And important things will take some time and effort. It may be that small steps are first steps – we are finding our feet before we can take bigger strides. Or it may be that in the busy hecticness of life, small steps are all we are going to be able to manage. But they need to be considered and purposeful small steps – so getting going will require a little push of effort.

We must be wary of seeing the scale or complexity of the problems around us and shutting down, stepping away and being overwhelmed. As we have said throughout this book, we do not need to despair, because these things are not ultimate. We are not going to find miraculous solutions, but the above steps are ways in which we can seek the welfare of the place in which we live, as ambassadors of Christ.

As you begin to enter into the world of local politics it is also worth doing the 'not in my back yard' or 'nimby' test. Are you happy to have strong values and believe that people should have adequate housing . . . unless it is anywhere near your house? Or are you happy to help out at a homeless shelter, but you wouldn't ever want to personally show people hospitality, or wouldn't be so charitable if it was your door they were sheltering in? We may need to check our motives; to make sure we are not getting involved for the sake of our egos and worthy ideals, but rather for the love of the people God created and cares for, and for the honour of his name.

Getting involved at a local level will probably take priority for most of us, but being informed about national politics is also important. There is much about central government that is incredibly frustrating. You might write a letter to your MP asking them to vote a certain way on a certain issue. They may reply; they may not. They then may vote the way you didn't want because of their party's position on the issue. Even if they do vote the way you asked, the Bill may pass when you wanted it to be defeated, or be defeated when you wanted it to pass.

But taking an interest is still important. Even if it doesn't feel as though a policy affects *you*, the chances are that it will affect someone in your community. Learning about an issue and understanding different points of view is essential. It is easy to jump in with our two pennies' worth as soon as we hear certain buzzwords. There is nothing that throws Christians into a mindless frenzy like the mention of life issues or sexuality. All nuance is rapidly lost, and everything becomes assertive opinions and stark black and white. We are not saying these aren't incredibly important issues, or that we should compromise our convictions on them. But we are saying that taking a bit of time to understand an issue, and showing care in how we express our views, will add a compassionate and considerate tone where it may otherwise be lacking.

Engaging with your politicians

We have looked at taking some small steps to get involved in politics. Now let's think about how we might engage with our politicians. Men and women employed in full-time politics are not the most popular bunch. People's instinctive response to politicians is often suspicion, and an assumption that they have self-interested ulterior motives. The other response is one of nervousness, an awkwardness, not wanting to ask about their work and what they are doing; possibly because we're worried they'll ask us to do something for them. But let's be honest, being a local councillor is not a very glamorous job; it is not well paid and involves navigating hard decisions, significant budget cuts and the impossible task of trying to please everyone.

Steph is a local councillor in Kingston upon Thames. She speaks of the pain and frustration of having to prioritize housing allocations – working out who has the greatest need when the waiting list is ten years long and there are countless desperate families. Or having to decide between closing children's centres or laying off health visitors in the face of budget cuts. It's a tough job and the vast majority of people who choose to do it are motivated by a desire to help their community.

Despite this, Steph has found the response from her church family somewhat mixed. While there is one couple who show an interest in what she is working on and pray for her regularly, people generally don't ask Steph about her political work, whether because of party leanings, general suspicion or nervousness.

As we think through the process of engaging with local politicians, a lot of the points are for churches and church leadership. But that doesn't mean they are not for us. Many of them can also be applied to our conduct as individuals. It also only takes one person to get the ball rolling. Busy church leaders often don't have the time and headspace to pause and re-evaluate how they interact with the community. So here are a few thoughts on how to engage with our politicians.

1 Build relationships with them. As a church, we should be supporting those in our church family who are involved in local or national politics and looking to them to guide us in how we might best serve our communities. This applies to all our politicians, not just those who attend our churches.

2 Let them know what you are doing as a church. Communicating with your politicians about what you are doing in the community can help them shape where they are putting resources as well as inform them of local needs.

3 Partner with them. Work in partnership for the sake of your community. Not only will it make you more effective but it is also an amazing witness.

4 Offer help rather than making demands. We need to come with humility. A lot of the decisions being made by politicians are very complex and difficult. A church will really stand out if it comes with the offer of help and support and not just a list of demands and expectations.

5 Find the common ground. Even if you are of different political persuasions and disagree with decisions that your politicians have made, remember that their role and purpose is to help the community. You will have common ground and common desires, even if sometimes you disagree on how to tackle the problem.

6 Keep them accountable. Keeping our local and national politicians accountable is really vital. It is important to identify areas that have been overlooked or inadequately provided for, or to make them aware of the impact of poor decisions. However, it is also important to try to work together to find solutions.

None of the things suggested in this chapter are rocket science, but nor are they a silver bullet for effortless political engagement. What this does give you is a place to start, and in many ways that first small step is the most important. So, pray these things through and look around you. Where has God placed you? How can he use you there? What is the passion and the heartbreak he has given you? Put some time in your diary to make that first step. It really matters.

And when you start to feel tired or discouraged, remember that Jesus sought justice on earth for the poor and the needy and those who were neglected by powerful rulers. He preached the salvation of souls, but he also got stuck in to the reality of the lives of the people around him. His currency was love, and it wasn't mushy and saccharine, but gritty and painful. He burst into a world of sickness and fear and fallen humanity, and it led him to the cross.

The story of the Bible is one where humans are called to reflect God's love to one another and look after the vulnerable. We are not called to sit back and wait for God to bestow blessings or thunderbolts. Christians throughout history have actively sought to change the world for the better and to work with God in bringing in his kingdom on earth as in heaven.

This is why we should get our hands dirty and not walk on by.

Case study: Steph Archer, local councillor

For Steph Archer, becoming a local councillor in Kingston in southwest London took a lifetime of gradual learning, and a moment's push. Her faith has grown since childhood through a painful family tragedy at a young age. Her faith caused her conviction for social justice to grow, and a CARE internship year in Tim Farron's office helped her to connect this passion for justice with legislative politics.

Working in Tim's office was an education in campaigning and engaging well in community politics. Naturally, Steph felt the need to address the problems she saw right around her. The local play park near to where she lived was in a terrible state. A good place to start. She gathered signatures for a petition. Began door knocking. The park was completely renovated as a result of her campaigning.

Then, a friend challenged her. Her work for the new park was essentially doing the work of a councillor – so why not actually be one? So she ran. In making this step she became the one who showed up. And when election day came around, she had a four-week-old baby in her arms and a seat on the local council.

Steph's reasons for running are simple. Loving, serving and giving. 'Being a local councillor is a really tangible way you can care and love your community.' While 'loving your neighbour' does mean loving *everyone*, it also means literally loving *your neighbours*, and caring for the area you share with them. The extra responsibilities and pressures of being a councillor are part of the sacrificial love you are showing your community. It is rarely easy to solve knotty local problems. The role requires time and effort and motivation, and often it is taken on alongside work or caring responsibilities or life commitments. It is a chance to serve, not to gain.

The sacrifices are worth it – 'there is such satisfaction' in being able to show this practical love, and, she points out, in seeing concrete change. Her experience seeing politics in Westminster was one of long, painfully slow change. It was hard to discern what real difference was being made in the more impersonal national picture. Whereas in local government 'you see change all the time'.

'Climate change and the biodiversity crisis feels so terrifying – yet as local councillors we can say, "Let's do a gardening project, let's bring in pollinators, let's invest in this green space and plant an orchard." We know there's a housing crisis – OK, so get involved in local politics and you can talk about building council housing in Kingston for the first time in thirty years. What an incredible thing to do!'

It can be so easy to look at the vast scale of a national or international problem, and despair. We are so small; the world and its systems are so deep and complex. Steph mentions climate change and the housing crisis, but it could be anything affecting your community. There is no way for anything to change without specific local change. 'It's grounded, it's able to make those differences, and I don't panic about the bigger issues.'

Steph's career as a councillor has not been dramatic, nor remarkable for epoch-shaking legislation, nor shaken by scandal. Just the calm and faithful service to her Kingston constituents. The temptation to panic or despair doesn't disappear, but 'knowing that we are doing our bit here … brings peace in the mayhem'.

12

By daring to pick a side

We hope that by reading this book Christians will be encouraged to seek to become more informed about politics; to pray, to understand the issues and to see why politics should matter deeply to Christians.

But we also hope that a handful of readers may feel called to take a further step: to stand for election to public office themselves. So what might this look like?

First, it is clear that Christians can, and do, legitimately hold a variety of different political views. In the UK, Christians find common cause with all the main parties. We do not all agree on some of the big issues – such as whether the government should invite more private companies to support the running of the NHS, or whether we should be building new airports or railway lines – and it is not wrong to be partisan in the right context. Sometimes, not picking a side means that we neglect to love our neighbour.

The reality of the UK political system is that if you want to be elected, you will be required to pick a side. You might be able to stand for local council as an independent candidate, but if you want to be in with a realistic chance of getting elected to Parliament or any of the devolved assemblies, you will need to nail your colours to a mast.

If you have never been party political, this might be daunting. Christians often have concerns about signing up to the whole range of policies and viewpoints that a party expresses. Signing up might make us feel we have to compromise our beliefs and our faith. But there are many Christians involved in the different parties, and it can be a rewarding and challenging experience.

How do I pick a side?

1 Do your research. There is a wealth of practical advice on the Christians in Politics website and the accompanying book, *Those Who Show Up* by Andy Flannagan. We don't want to repeat it all here, so we would encourage you to take a look.

The Christians in Politics website and the UCCF Politics Network both offer downloads of resources that look in depth at the principles of the main political parties and their links to Christianity.[1] The websites of the parties themselves set out many of their policies. The main parties also have active Christian organizations within them.[2] Explore their websites and Twitter feeds, and find out what they believe and how they would address the issues that you care about.

Talk to people you know who are already active or interested in politics. Often people are drawn towards a particular party not because they agree with all its manifesto policies but because they have good relationships with people who support it or campaign for it. There are great people within all the parties, and if you get involved, they can truly feel like a family.

2 Don't expect to agree with any party on every issue. We don't all agree with members of our church on every issue. We don't even agree with members of our family on everything! Political parties are broad coalitions of people who come together with a variety of agendas and passions to work for a common cause.

Over the years, there have been overtly Christian parties that have stood for election across the UK. However, we would encourage you to join one of the main parties, as this is where you are most

---

1   <www.christiansinpolitics.org.uk/books-guides> (accessed 13 July 2022).
2   Conservative Christian Fellowship (<www.theccf.co.uk>); Christians on the Left (<www.christiansontheleft.org.uk>); Liberal Democrat Christian Forum (<www.ldcf.org>).

likely to have influence and impact. One of the disadvantages of having a 'Christian party' is that Christians have a variety of beliefs and viewpoints. We are not a homogeneous group, and Christians have never identified with a single party in the UK. In addition, our 'two party' political system hugely favours the Labour and Conservative parties, so it is difficult for smaller parties to gain seats at general elections. There are other parties that tend to be middle-sized at Westminster; for instance, the Liberal Democrats in my time have had as few as 8 MPs and as many as 63. Likewise, the SNP has had as many as 56 and as few as 6. At each election, there is a myriad of small parties that stand, but few of them make an impact. In recent years, the UK Independence Party (UKIP) and then the Brexit Party have gained a good deal of support for standing on single issues, which speaks volumes about the resonance of the Brexit issue, but it is notable that they have still failed to win seats at general elections.

As Andy Flannagan points out, it is more effective for us to be salt and light throughout society and within the established political parties than it is to withdraw into our own silos and just talk to one another. He asks: 'What if instead of forming separate cultures or industries we allowed more of the God-given creativity of believers to infuse the mainstream?[3]

3 *Look beyond the stereotypes.* If you look at the news headlines, or identify with a particular 'tribe' in our current culture wars, it's likely that you will be encouraged to view politics in black and white. This is exacerbated when parties become polarized within their own ranks.

Detractors will focus on what they dislike about their opponents, while high-profile politicians provoke controversies that further damage the reputation of politics in general. But personalities come

---

3   Andy Flannagan, *Those Who Show Up* (Edinburgh: Muddy Pearl, 2015), p. 58.

and go, and while 'Tory', 'socialist' and 'liberal' can all be used as derogatory terms, the underlying issues and principles are generally far more complex and nuanced than the headlines suggest.

Former MP David Burrowes gives a thorough defence of Conservative values for the UCCF Politics Network.[4] He sets out that conservatism is driven by a desire to conserve the best of the past, building on the wisdom of institutions and authorities through which we hold stewardship of the earth in trust from God. Conservatism believes in the dignity of the individual while at the same time recognizing that humanity is fallen. It emphasizes the freedom that God gives us to decide how to use our talents and our wealth. This brings with it responsibility to the poor, and Conservatives believe that care and wealth redistribution should be done freely by individuals and organizations such as the church, family and other voluntary institutions, rather than by compulsion from the state.

Labour MP Rachael Maskell has written in support of socialism, also for the Politics Network. She says:

> Socialism itself seeks to ensure that no individual is left behind. It reaches out to all, not least the most vulnerable, and sews a safety net beneath them to protect them and then raises it up to help advance their lives; journeying together to improve the conditions of all in society.[5]

Socialism seeks to break down the structural barriers that hold people back from achieving their potential – such as poverty and inequality. It takes a collective approach, encouraging the organization of people into groups, such as unions to protect workers and seek better conditions for them. It emphasizes the importance

---

4   <https://politicsnetwork.uk/think/the-christian-case-for-conservatism> (accessed 11 July 2022).
5   <https://politicsnetwork.uk/think/the-christian-case-for-socialism> (accessed 11 July 2022).

of state involvement to address these structural issues and create a fairer society.

As for liberalism, there is a particular hang-up for many evangelical-leaning Christians who sometimes confuse liberal theology and liberal politics. We feel that it is important to straighten out this confusion and have written further about this in appendix A. British liberalism has a long history and was founded in the battle for religious liberty. Nonconformist Christian groups were persecuted in the eighteenth century by a society that favoured adherence only to the established church. In response, they built a liberal movement that championed much wider liberty – for women, for cultural and regional minorities, and for the poor and vulnerable. Today, liberalism can have an intolerant edge to it, but at its heart it is an ideology that permits the flourishing of different values and world views. It defends the right of people to exist – free from poverty, ignorance or conformity – alongside one another in a plural society. It emphasizes social justice and care for the environment, and seeks a balance between liberty, equality and community.

This is a very brief summary of the distinctive beliefs of the main national political parties. Of course, Scotland, Wales and Northern Ireland all have a wider range of parties, whose websites you can investigate further.[6]

Which political party best reflects your own outlook and priorities?

4 Ask yourself whether you can work well with the people involved, seeking common goals. Christians in Politics suggests you ask yourself three questions before you join a party:

---

6   SNP member Neil Macleod makes the case for nationalism in the context of Scottish independence for UCCF here: <https://politicsnetwork.uk/think/the-christian-case-for-nationalism> (accessed 11 July 2022). You can find links to the websites of all the parties represented in the UK Parliament here: <www.parliament.uk/about/mps-and-lords/members/parties> (accessed 11 July 2022).

1 Do I want to serve my community?
2 Can I work with people I may not wholly agree with for the common good?
3 Do I feel God can use me to influence politics from within the system rather than just from the outside?[7]

Ultimately, politics is about people working together towards common aims, and it is important that you are able to cooperate with others. As in any group of people working together, this will involve debate, disagreement and, yes, sometimes compromise. But we often find we have more influence when we knuckle down and get involved on the inside.

5 Remember: political parties do not command your ultimate loyalty. The principle of collective responsibility means that MPs, and particularly government ministers, are expected to stand behind the stated policies and aims of their parties. On the whole, it is best to get involved in the debates while the policies are in the process of being formed. Policymaking works differently in different parties. In the Liberal Democrats, for example, there are opportunities for members to sit on policy working groups, to shape party policy and to debate motions at the party's spring and autumn conferences.

However, ultimately, as Christians we must put Kingdom before Tribe. Political parties are not our gods; they will let us down. Sometimes we may feel obliged to oppose our party line on an issue. MPs sometimes vote against their whip. Conscience issues, including abortion and assisted dying, still command 'free votes' in the House of Commons, where MPs are not expected to follow a party line, although there is often social pressure on them to vote in a certain way.

---

7 <www.christiansinpolitics.org.uk/the-tragedy-and-possibility-of-joining-a-political-party> (accessed 11 July 2022).

How to get elected

The actual process of selection and election varies between parties, and it is best to seek advice directly from each party on the practicalities.

But everyone has a unique story of his or her journey to selection and election. The Mucky Business podcast gives an insight into some of these, as we interview MPs from across the political spectrum.

Practicalities

Once you have decided which party to join, the best way to get your hands dirty is to get involved in your local branch or constituency party. To find your local party, type the name of your constituency and the party you would like to join into the search engine of your choice. It should provide you with contact details.[8]

Then turn up to meetings, offer to deliver leaflets, knock on doors. This may lead to someone asking you to take on a key role in the local party quite quickly. Enthusiasm and reliability are greatly valued and it is very important to build relationships and earn trust. You should also get involved with the Christian organization within your party, as these groups offer support and advice to prospective candidates for any level of office.

Politics can be hard work and it can be lonely. As addressed earlier, it will throw up many temptations and opportunities to compromise, for good or for ill. It is also likely to open you up to criticism and abuse from people you have never met.

---

8   To find out which constituency you live in, type your postcode into the search engine on the Parliament website: <https://members.parliament.uk/constituencies> (accessed 11 July 2022).

How to respond to abuse

In chapter 10 we talk about the importance of praying for politicians and seeing them as people too, and the inevitable exposure to loss and rejection, vilification and even violence. We could add to that the recent murders of two MPs in the line of duty: Jo Cox and David Amess.

We have talked about the importance of how we relate to politicians (e.g. by not giving them abuse), but what if you want to become a politician yourself? How should you approach the reality that you will receive, not just criticism, but quite probably abuse – mostly on social media but also in person? Women and minorities tend to receive even more abuse than white men. And perhaps we feel that expressing views as a Christian will expose us to this even more.

I don't want to sound blasé, but I think I've received two or maybe three credible death threats during my time; the police dealt brilliantly with them. I am grateful to God not only that I remained safe but also that I never let those threats get under my skin or unnerve me.

I have, however, been deeply upset and driven almost to depression by online and other derision that I have received. We might say that in my case, sticks and stones broke no bones but the words really hurt me.

No way would I compare the verbal and written grief I have received with the genuine persecution faced by Christians in other countries, but it's still unpleasant. So what are we talking about here and how might we deal with it?

We are likely to face opposition if we are in public life and hold to what the Bible says about, for example, sex, sexuality, and the sanctity of life at every age. Even if we don't wish to legislate to enact those views in law, we may be branded as hateful bigots. If we hold that God created all things, that there is such a thing as sin, that we will be judged by that almighty God, that we aren't our own, we may be branded judgmental. If we believe in a God at all and trust what the Bible says about him, we may be branded as credulous idiots. Bigoted, judgmental idiots. If you aren't upset by people thinking that sort of thing about you, then you have less of a pride problem than I do!

In response to even my best-liked tweet, there will be someone who replies with 'Shut up, homophobe!' or something similar. This crushes me, to be honest, because my self-image is as someone who is kind, understanding, faithful to God and loving towards my neighbour. In reality I am rubbish at all those things, but to be thought of as a bigot gets to me. I hate it.

So how do we deal with this kind of thing?

First practical tip: try not to engage online with people who are just being insulting. In my experience, those attacks are from people who aren't at the stage of wanting a genuine discussion or to listen to any nuance. Don't pour petrol on the fire. Leave them alone and don't reply.

Second, it's OK to keep off social media. We can often think that 'everyone thinks X about me', but no, they don't! A few dozen people we are unlikely to meet have said something horrible, but in reality 99.9% of the country is blissfully unaware of whatever controversy it is. Get out of the small box-room that is social media and walk out into the wide-open space beyond it.

Third, though, in the long term don't hide away. I hold hundreds of opinions. Most of them I hope are biblically inspired in some way, and so I don't think I easily fit into any specific 'culture war' bubble. As a result, people who hate the fact that I think we must take seriously what the Bible says about sex may also be hugely positive about what I think on the issue of showing generosity to refugees. It might cause their heads to explode, but the more we persevere in being rounded Christians, engaging across the range of issues, the more people will see that dismissing us as 'bigoted, judgmental idiots' just doesn't compute.

In some cases it might be wise, for our mental health, to block certain people on social media or to avoid engaging on a personal level . . . but I have very rarely done that. In fact, I have deliberately made a point of following people who strongly disagree with me, or engaging positively with a rare post of theirs that I agree with.

This kind of approach – I hope – means that when I do get into a position where I can present the gospel, they might just listen. I also mean it to be a good witness, to be kind and even light with people who aren't like that with me. I don't always succeed in this!

Whether it be in person, on the phone, through second-hand gossip or online, the individuals who defame us are made in God's image and are both accountable to God and worthy to be loved by us as our neighbour.

Easier said than done, I know. Andy Flannagan in his book *Those Who Show Up* encourages Christians seeking to enter politics to consider carefully and practically who they will ask to accompany them on their journey into a political role.[9] He is absolutely right. Christians should not enter politics alone. When I was first elected as an MP I had a small fellowship group in my constituency; one friend who was a member called it 'Tim's hovercraft' because its job was to lift me up above deep water!

We need people to pray for us and with us, but we also need fellow Christians to join us in the endeavour. Not everyone on our campaign team needs to be a Christian, but some of them should be. It is good to have brothers and sisters in Christ to pray for us, hear us and care for us, but it is even better to have Christians who will also understand our political work by being part of it themselves too.

As we say elsewhere, one of those prayers to which God promises to give an unequivocal 'yes' is the prayer for wisdom. Do pray for wisdom. For wisdom to say what is right, to respond graciously, and to decide when silence or discretion could be the best course of action.

---

9   Flannagan, *Those Who Show Up*, ch. 16, pp. 182–188.

In Matthew's Gospel, Jesus tells us: 'Blessed are you when people insult you, persecute you and falsely say all kinds of evil against you because of me. Rejoice and be glad, because great is your reward in heaven' (Matthew 5:11–12). As Christians, then, we should expect some of any abuse that we receive to be 'because of him' and the work that we're seeking to do in his name.

That doesn't mean we should seek out confrontation, arguments and vilification. But when it does come, we must turn to God for our strength, perspective, confidence and affirmation.

In order to get firmly involved in politics, we know that it's necessary to pick a side. But we should also remember not to become tribal in those choices. Instead, we should hold them lightly, graciously understand other perspectives and criticisms, and in doing so take the opportunity to be a very different kind of politician for Jesus' sake.

Other ways to get involved

If you have a heart for certain issues or for the process of government, but do not feel called to join a party, there are many other ways to get involved in the public square without actually campaigning or standing for election. These options include:

- *The civil service.* Government departments and agencies are staffed by politically independent officials who assist the government of the day in developing and implementing its policies.[10]
- *Charities and NGOs (non-governmental organizations).* There are many groups which lobby government on particular issues where they want to see change in society, tackling subjects as diverse as cancer, poverty and sustainable transport.[11]

---

10 <www.gov.uk/government/organisations/civil-service/about> (accessed 11 July 2022).
11 <https://jobs.theguardian.com/article/how-to-get-a-job-at-a-charity> (accessed 11 July 2022).

- *Think tanks.* These organizations carry out research and produce reports and policy recommendations on a wide range of issues, through which they aim to influence government and political parties.[12]

Conclusion

If any of this resonates with you, and you feel God may be calling you to active involvement in politics, then pray about it, seek support, get stuck in . . . and let us know your story!

Case study: Rosie Farron

Where to start?

When Tim got elected as the MP for Westmorland and Lonsdale in May 2005, I was elated and gobsmacked in equal measure as I never believed it would actually happen. The reality set in very quickly as, having been up for most of the night, Tim had to go into Kendal and I had to look after our younger children, who were aged three and one at the time, on next to no sleep. It was a kind of giddy journey because lots of people were so pleased about Tim's election and we were stopped often to be congratulated. Since then, it's been seventeen years, for two of which he was Leader.

To give a snapshot of what it's like to be an MP's wife over that period of time is challenging. There are obviously highs and lows. It's an immense privilege and I love the fact that my husband is fighting for the things that I believe in and doing a really good job of it. From the other side, it has its drawbacks as it can be lonely, more so when the children were younger. That said, Tim is a brilliant dad and has always made time for the children, and we go

---

12 <https://smartthinking.org.uk/the-think-tanks> (accessed 11 July 2022).

on some lovely holidays, mainly in the UK (well, Scotland based), but in the summer, as time allows, to France or Spain.

We've been guests at some very special events, the highlight of which was a dinner at Buckingham Palace in July 2017 to welcome the king of Spain. That was a challenge for me as it was to be hosted midweek, in the middle of my workdays. I told my line manager and our faculty dean that I'd been invited (with Tim obviously) and they were incredulous when I said that I couldn't go for two reasons: 1) because of when it fell, and 2) because I didn't have enough leave. They persuaded me to swap my days, and our oldest daughter, Izzie, agreed to look after the younger three. It was an immense privilege and I met some amazing people. I wouldn't change that experience for any other.

The downside was being the 'Leader's wife'. I allowed myself to be convinced that I had to have an official photo taken at the party conference in Bournemouth in September 2015, even though I really didn't want to. The press lived up to my cynical view of them by printing an unpleasant headline about my 'rictus' smile; I actually had to look that word up and I was so cross when I realized what it meant that I emailed the editor of *The Observer* to express my distaste. I did get a reply, only to be told that I was fair game as I'd agreed to the photograph!

I've been a lot more private ever since, but being an MP's wife is still a privilege.

13

By loving our neighbour and standing firm

Let's suppose that you decide to join a political party or become a member of your parish council. Or perhaps you start volunteering for a charity supporting older people, for a mental health group, or for an organization providing support and counselling for people living with cancer. You choose to do this because you see that by involving yourself in your community, you can love your neighbour in a practical way by meeting people's needs and showing compassion for them. You also know that by being in the same place as your neighbour, you are much more likely to find an opportunity to share the gospel than if you are not.

This is where your challenge will begin!

To state the obvious, the world we live in does not recognize Jesus as Lord. The values of the organizations we join will not, on the whole, be consciously shaped by the Christian faith. So how do we relate to others who do not share our faith when we involve ourselves in those organizations? How do we relate to those we are able to help and support through our activism, if they don't share our beliefs?

Some non-Christians may have very different lifestyles from us, certain aspects of which we might consider to be in opposition to what the Bible teaches. However, in some cases, our reaction to those lifestyle differences might just be down to our own quirks and habits, which owe more to tradition and church culture than they do to biblical teaching!

For some Christians, considerations about how non-Christians are 'different' don't really occur to them. If we are of this mindset, we don't expect the majority of people we come across to be Christians in the first place, so we're not surprised when they're not. We live our lives mostly around non-believers whose days are lived to a different beat and to different standards and values, yet we don't think of ourselves as being very different from others. And in one sense we are right to think that. We are no better or worse than non-Christians. We are sinners just like them, and we are created in the image of God just like them – in desperate need of forgiveness and yet fundamentally awesome and precious image-bearing creations of the Almighty!

In another sense, we *are* quite different. In John's Gospel, Jesus tells us: 'whoever hears my word and believes . . . will not be judged but has crossed over from death to life' (John 5:24). To put it bluntly, there are no two beings more different than one which is alive and one which is dead!

I am one of those whose default position is as described above – given that most of my interactions are with people who are not Christians. My default position is to breeze along, not really thinking about our differences. Sometimes this can make me a less than effective witness to others because I fear – consciously or otherwise – that to live publicly for Christ would be off-putting and might disrupt comfortable relationships with colleagues and volunteers.

Other Christians, however, will feel the distinction with non-Christians much more sharply and might then be much more reluctant to get involved in civil society in the first place. If they do get involved, they may be far more nervous about their activism. What about when we come across people whose lifestyles are in opposition to God's way? How do we treat people whose entire world view is different from ours? Are we going to look as though we 'approve' of unchristian lifestyles if we don't 'say something'? More generally, do we risk losing our saltiness if we immerse ourselves too deeply in secular activities and organizations?

In short, how do we stand firm in our faith in Christ, yet love the people we encounter through our volunteering or activism?

Who are these sinners?

Jesus did not live a monastic lifestyle. We don't have a record of much of Jesus' life on earth, but the New Testament accounts show that his life was lived in public and in community. He socialized with people of low social standing, and who were outside the religious leadership, at least as much as he did with those of high status. Jesus talked with pious and powerful people, and he also ate with tax collectors and sinners. In other words, he invested time with individuals who were deemed traitors to and exploiters of their own people, and also with individuals who were living outside the religious laws of the day. To be more precise, this will have included people who were backsliders, irreligious non-observing Jews, and hedonists of various kinds – people whose lives would be thought 'immoral'.

He also ate with Pharisees, teachers of the law and priests – people who would have been considered highly respectable and good. Sometimes he was with these insiders and outsiders at the same time. A bit like when, as a student, I invited my band mates and my political mates to the same party. Really awkward . . .

Jesus came across a huge number of people, some of whom we know about. In one passage, we see that Jesus encounters a woman who has been bleeding for twelve years and would have been utterly isolated and shunned for this, and then – at pretty much the same time – a synagogue ruler called Jairus whose daughter is dying.

The outsider and the insider both throw themselves on the mercy of Jesus. The insider, albeit humbly and respectfully, has the confidence to approach Jesus for help, yet the outsider can only bring herself to touch Jesus' cloak, hoping to be healed and at the same time not to be noticed. Jesus helps them both.

Jesus and his disciples did not seem to discriminate when it came to choosing who they spent their time with. High and low. Good and bad. Respectable and despised. All were welcome to dinner, or to a quiet chat one to one.

Jesus didn't detour around any groups or any types of person. That's a useful clue as to how we should order our interactions.

We see Jesus healing and directly intervening in the lives of many people from diverse backgrounds. The religious and the irreligious, Jews, Samaritans, Romans and more. Yet we also see him teaching and in discussion with a multitude.

Jesus never approved of or endorsed lifestyles that were in opposition to the Bible's teaching. But when he chastised people, it was almost always relating to their failure to acknowledge their sin, their need of a saviour, or their blindness to who he is.

If that is how Jesus behaved around non-believers, then surely we should follow suit? Yes, mostly. But then again, we are not Jesus. He is perfect. Therefore, when he chides or chastises, he is not being a hypocrite. Also, there was no question with Jesus that being alongside 'sinners' would rub off on him and he would become a bit less righteous. For us, there is that challenge. We want to serve our neighbours (and in doing so, honour God) by, let's say, being alongside them volunteering for a political party, an environmental pressure group or a homelessness charity. We don't want to alienate those around us; we see them as nice, decent people; they live lives without God . . . and do you know what? It just doesn't seem that bad. Why the fuss? Before long, we might find ourselves considering the Bible's teaching on matters of family, respect for parents, chastity outside marriage, gossip, judging others and so on to be just a bit po-faced and unreasonable.

So what's the answer? The answer is to see the non-Christians we serve, and those we serve alongside, as Jesus saw them: 'When he saw the crowds, he had compassion on them, because they were harassed and helpless, like sheep without a shepherd' (Matthew 9:36). We can often see the lifestyles of others as glamorous and more attractive and exciting than ours, but we shouldn't. If you've ever read *The Screwtape Letters* by C. S. Lewis, you'll probably, like me, have nodded knowingly at how the devil's schemes normally involve getting the believer or the potential believer to see the grass on the other side as greener. It's so simple, clever and effective – so we need to pray for eyes that see that deceit every time and to be always on our guard. That person who is sleeping with his girlfriend, takes drugs, makes people laugh by gossiping about others – you need to see him as he really is, as Jesus sees him: not having the fun life that you are missing out on, but harassed and helpless . . . and in desperate need of a shepherd. You are the one who can point that person to the shepherd. You'll need to prepare and pray for the right time and opportunity to do the pointing.

There will be people and places that a Christian should avoid. Jesus spent time with sinners, but then again he was the sinless one, uniquely pure. We are not, and so we will sometimes need to 'pluck out our right eye in case it offends us' (see Matthew 5:29); we may sometimes need to hide, to remove ourselves from a situation if it runs a risk of leading us into sin. If we can keep faithful to God by serving non-Christians and by working shoulder to shoulder with them, we certainly should – but we should be wise in how we handle ourselves.

How can we stand firm as we seek to love our neighbour in practical ways? First, we should pray about that service and the situations it leads us into and the people we spend time with. Let's pray daily and ask others to pray for us and with us. We should ask for protection from temptation, for opportunities to share the gospel, for the success of the projects we are working on and for God to give us a loving, sacrificial sincerity in our service.

Second, we need to make sure that we are embedded in fellowship with other Christians. That means regular small-group togetherness where we can speak openly about our voluntary work, express our concerns and fears, and talk these over with brothers and sisters in Christ. This helps us to keep our motives under review, to be accountable and to receive encouragement in the work we are doing.

Third, when we volunteer, we don't need to declare our moral position on everything out of a paranoid fear that, if we don't, we are somehow approving of something God considers to be wrong. Instead, let us be clear – but gentle – in 'outing' ourselves as Christians early on. The 'What did you do at the weekend?' question will eventually lead to the return question, which allows us to explain that we went to church. Or during discussions about what we did last night, we will get the chance to say we were at house group . . . and then to explain what we do there.

Then we need to think about responses to the normal replies we will get to this, some of which will be a little awkward and defensive, or self-deprecating, or politely misinformed ('I think I'm a good Christian – I try to live a good life'; 'I wish I had faith . . . I respect people who do', etc.), to which we need to prepare a gentle response that leads to further good conversations later. For instance, 'I'm a Christian because I know I'm *not* a good person', or 'If you think about it, we all put our faith in lots of things each day – faith is just trusting someone or something, normally on the basis of some evidence that shows us it's safe to do so'.

In 1 Peter 3:15 we are told: 'Always be prepared to give an answer to everyone who asks you to give the reason for the hope that you have. But do this with gentleness and respect.'

I think this means that we should prepare our answers, to make ourselves ready in advance for those occasions when we are asked. Of course, always approaching every situation with gentleness and respect. So, when someone lives a lifestyle that is in opposition to God's perfect plan for human beings (and we have all done so, remember), then our response should be gentle and respectful. We don't need to contradict that person all the time or skirt around the subject. People are who they are at that point in time, and they're not going to be any more open to the gospel if we are silently 'tutting' or being awkward around them. Love them, pray for opportunities, and demonstrate that gentleness and respect.

In his book *The Prodigal God*, Tim Keller examines Jesus' famous parable and outlines that all of us sinners are essentially either the younger son or the older son – or maybe a bit of both. We're flagrantly disobedient, disregarding rules, disbelieving in God – we're rebels against our Father in heaven. Or else, we are terribly obedient, we are proud of our righteousness, and we are sniffy and full of condemnation about those we consider to be breaking the rules or not being as righteous as we are. The older, 'good' son sounds like lots of religious people we could think of, but he also sounds rather like a lot of terribly self-righteous non-Christians too!

How does the father in that parable react to both of those sons? With love and with patience. He isn't irritated or angry; he keeps waiting and waiting for the rebel to return; he is full of love and compassion. When the righteous son protests, the father puts an arm around him and pleads with him; there is no sharp rebuke. At the same time, the father never accepts that either son has reacted in an appropriate way. So it should be with us. We should seek to be patient, to keep loving those we spend time with, keep praying for them and preparing our words, keep talking about our work with Christian brothers and sisters, and involve them in our thinking and our experiences. We should always pray for love and sincerity in our service, that our motives would be pure and rooted in a desire to love others as we have been loved by God – sacrificially and without condition.

Case study: Dr Lisa Cameron MP

Dr Lisa Cameron is a consultant clinical psychologist who, by some unexpected turns of events, became SNP MP for East Kilbride, Strathaven and Lesmahagow. Twelve months before the 2015 election she was not even a member of the SNP but, like many, became the candidate to give the local SNP branch a good showing, and ended up winning. As the campaign went on, and the polls were looking good for the SNP, Lisa's mum bought her a present – a travel hairdryer. She said: 'I think you're going to be needing this.' She was right!

Lisa has taken on a role in Parliament as a consensus-builder. She chairs All-Party Parliamentary Groups (APPGs), including the high-profile Health APPG. These roles require an ability to calmly allow respectful disagreement and debate. In the often bitter and divisive debates about Scotland's future in or out of the UK, Lisa uses the skills and principles she acquired in her former career as an NHS psychologist. 'Really my job was to listen and understand people and their points of view. That's always at the root of building any agreement or consensus.' Lisa's example is a great witness to Paul's encouragement in Philippians 4:5 (ESV): 'Let your reasonableness be known to everyone.'

According to Lisa, any interaction with people 'must come from that position of respect ... of other people's views. You're not always going to agree with other people, but you have to be courteous, you have to listen and you have to try to understand their viewpoints too ... Unless we do that, we can't represent everyone in the constituency.'

This means that for Lisa, even the defining division line of Scottish politics – the stance on independence – comes second to a constituent's needs. 'I have gone the extra mile to make sure that no matter the constitutional division in people's minds, they can still come to me as their MP and I will try to represent them to the best of my abilities.' These principles are crucial beyond even Parliament and constituency matters. 'Fundamentally, that's important in terms of my views of the world, my Christian beliefs, and also my work as an NHS psychologist.'

Lisa voted, in a conscience vote, against extending Westminster abortion law over Northern Ireland. She was, she admits, 'quite naively surprised at the level of vitriol' she received; she was sent hundreds and hundreds of messages arguing that she should not stand again for Parliament after voting the way she did. It put her staff and family under immense stress in the immediate backlash after the vote. 'It made such an impact on those around me that I was beginning to think: *Can I be myself in Parliament? Can I hold the beliefs I have and maintain my integrity?*'

There was, however, also an 'outpouring' of support from people right across the UK and even from Christians all over the world grateful for her taking a stand. 'It was so heartening and gave me such belief.' This shows that writing to Christian MPs with encouragement is a powerful form of fellowship that has a real impact at some of the most difficult moments in their career. For Lisa, it gave her 'real courage to continue' after the initial wobbles and doubts.

Lisa's career has already exemplified how Christians in politics can be like Jesus, loving and standing 'full of grace and truth' (John 1:14). Having grace in how we interact with one another, especially those with whom we may disagree viscerally. Sticking to the truth with humility, kindness and love, even when it invites a backlash.

14

By keeping the eternal perspective in mind

Humans have always wondered about the nature of time and the point of existence. It is a theme that runs through our literature. One of Percy Bysshe Shelley's most famous poems describes a ruined statue in the desert. Clearly once a mighty monument to a formidable king, now just the legs and broken face remain, and an inscription at the base:

> And on the pedestal, these words appear:
> My name is Ozymandias, King of Kings;
> Look on my Works, ye Mighty, and despair!
> Nothing beside remains. Round the decay
> Of that colossal Wreck, boundless and bare
> The lone and level sands stretch far away.[1]

The Egyptian pharaoh Ramses II (Ozymandias in Greek) was also known as Ramses the Great. He ruled the Nineteenth Dynasty in the thirteenth century BC, but today little is left of his powerful 'works', which have dissolved back into the desert. Shelley is reflecting on the transience of power: though they may wield enormous influence in their time, even the greatest empires and most powerful rulers fade and vanish and are forgotten.

For obvious reasons, the dramas and crises of the present always feel much more relevant to us than historical events. On one hand,

---

1   Percy Bysshe Shelley, 'Ozymandias', 1818.

the past offers us the benefit of hindsight, knowing how the story ended – or at least how it transitioned into the next set of circumstances. It also puts us at a safe distance from the incidents that are described. We may empathize with those who suffered in the past, and we may stop to consider how we might have been affected had we lived during those days, but we generally have the freedom to shudder and move on. On the other hand, we simply don't know exactly how the current issues affecting our country, our planet and our politics will pan out, and our lack of knowledge and control can be unsettling and make us anxious.

There is so much need in the world, so much anger and conflict, and the story of today is still being told. It is easy to feel engulfed by everything we think we ought to be doing to make changes in our hurting world, and this book may even have added to that feeling for some readers. This is why in this chapter we are taking a step back to consider the eternal perspective. God knows the end of the story, and he promises that the best is yet to come.

There are times when we feel thoroughly overwhelmed. Back in 2019 when the Brexit debates were taking place in Parliament, the atmosphere around Westminster, as well as across the UK, was heavy and tense. You would get into a lift with a group of MPs all looking solemn and deeply weary, and on some occasions close to tears. Everyone on both sides of the debate was deeply emotionally invested in what was taking place, and this intensity of feeling radiated out across the country. Then came the Covid-19 pandemic . . .

Three UK lockdowns, and frightening rates of hospital admissions and deaths all took their toll. Schools were closed to most pupils for two prolonged periods, and most of us hunkered down in our homes. The whole world felt overwhelmed by the pandemic. But as millions of people were vaccinated, and even with the emergence of new variants, hospital and death rates started falling, restrictions were lifted and we started to see light at the end of the dark tunnel. But at the time of writing in 2022, we still don't know how long it will take to reach the exit, or what the rest of the journey will look like – or what will be the final cost to lives, livelihoods and mental health.

Now we have entered a new geopolitical crisis after Vladimir Putin ordered the invasion of Ukraine in February 2022. Once more, the media is full of tales of horror, and fears of nuclear war loom again for the first time since the end of the Cold War. We simply do not know how the coming weeks and months will play out.

The Bible tells many stories about hard times when God's people felt overwhelmed and frightened by events around them. But these stories all carry a message of hope in the darkness, and the promise of a time when evil and suffering will be overcome.

By the rivers of Babylon . . .

The prophet Jeremiah lived at the height of the powerful, predatory Babylonian Empire. During this period, the kingdom of Judah was conquered by King Nebuchadnezzar, and many of the Jewish people were taken into exile in Babylon. Psalm 137 is a song of the exiles, singing and weeping as they remember their lost homes. Yet Jeremiah (ch. 50) prophesied that Babylon would fall. He proclaimed that the great city would be plundered, laid waste and deserted, so that only wild animals would dwell there. Doubtless those around him, observing the mighty works of the Babylonian Empire, would have ridiculed him for these words. Yet only a few decades later, in 539 BC, as recorded in the book of Daniel, the Persians under King Cyrus the Great conquered this mighty empire.

When we read the book of Revelation, there are multiple references to Babylon, although it had been in ruins for centuries at this point. Babylon is symbolic of every empire or set of circumstances that rises, burns brightly for a while and eventually falls into desolation. But Babylon was particularly symbolic for the early Christians who first read Revelation: it represented mighty, oppressive, murderous Rome, which was now the dominant world empire. And

Rome at this time was persecuting Christians, impoverishing them and ridiculing them. It was sending them into the arena to be eaten alive by wild animals. But, the author of Revelation reminded them, mighty Rome would go the same way as mighty Babylon.

And sure enough, the site of ancient Babylon and the historical centre of Rome are both now Unesco World Heritage sites. Rather than cowering and trembling before these human empires, we patronize them with a guidebook and a camera.

Indeed, Daniel foresaw the fall of both these empires, when God gave him the interpretation of Nebuchadnezzar's dream. And the small stone that came seemingly from nowhere and smashed them to pieces would be from God, and it would herald 'a kingdom that will never be destroyed, nor will it be left to another people. It will crush all those kingdoms and bring them to an end, but it will itself endure for ever' (Daniel 2:44). This stone was Jesus, and his kingdom endures.

Whenever we feel overwhelmed by the enormity of events or of pressures, we might look up to the sky. The introduction to the 1979 bestselling novel *The Hitch Hiker's Guide to the Galaxy* tells us: 'Space is big. Really big. You just won't believe how vastly, hugely, mind-bogglingly big it is. I mean, you may think it's a long way down the road to the chemist, but that's just peanuts to space.'[2] In case we are slightly overwhelmed by this idea, the front cover of the book gives a helpful instruction in big friendly letters: 'Don't Panic'.

Don't panic. It is all temporary. This is the hope we are offered. God is sovereign. He was on the throne then and he is on the throne now. He will be on the throne for evermore. The European Union, Brexit Britain, Putin's Russia and the Covid-19 pandemic will all fade and fall into rubble. So when we are tempted to fear the enormity of world events, of wars and plagues and matters beyond our control, we must remember not to panic.

---

2   Douglas Adams, *The Hitch Hiker's Guide to the Galaxy: A Trilogy in Five Parts*, collected edn (London: William Heinemann, 1995), p. 63.

The psalmist used the awesomeness of space as a reason to find comfort and reassurance:

> When I consider your heavens,
>> the work of your fingers,
> the moon and the stars,
>> which you have set in place,
> what is mankind that you are mindful of them,
>> human beings that you care for them?
> (Psalm 8:3–4)

In 2 Corinthians 4:18, Paul tells us to fix our eyes not on what is temporary but on the unseen eternal hope that we have in Jesus.

But we must not make the mistake of thinking that because all these things are temporary, they are all meaningless and what we do on earth does not matter.

The book of Ecclesiastes makes this point powerfully by throwing into question everything humans have valued down the ages:

> What do people gain from all their labours
>> at which they toil under the sun?
> Generations come and generations go,
>> but the earth remains for ever . . .
> No one remembers the former generations,
>> and even those yet to come
> will not be remembered
>> by those who follow them.
> (Ecclesiastes 1:3–4, 11)

Do we think our lives matter, our relationships are significant? Do we think there is something new under the sun? Something worthwhile to live for? If we do, we are kidding ourselves, says Ecclesiastes. *If there is no God*, it is all utterly meaningless.

Shakespeare put a similar idea into the despairing mouth of Macbeth:

> Life's but a walking shadow, a poor player
> That struts and frets his hour upon the stage
> And then is heard no more: it is a tale
> Told by an idiot, full of sound and fury,
> Signifying nothing.
> (*Macbeth*, Act 5, Scene 5)

The Bible has much to say about how ephemeral our lives are. Psalm 103 reminds us that our lives are like grass: a human life will flourish briefly like a flower, but then 'the wind blows over it and it is gone, and its place remembers it no more' (v. 16). But instead of concluding, like Macbeth, that it signifies nothing, we are offered the hope that

> from everlasting to everlasting
>   the LORD's love is with those who fear him . . .
> The LORD has established his throne in heaven,
>   and his kingdom rules over all.
> (Psalm 103:17, 19)

Either there is an almighty God, there is right and wrong, and there is purpose in this chaotic world of ours, or there is nothing, in which case nothing matters. Our lives are temporary; our achievements are all pointless. They will die with us, and the world on which we are buried will eventually be burned up. The universe will fizzle out and nothing will remain.

Ironically, many atheists, denying the existence of God, behave as though their lives have significance. But if they are right, they simply don't. And many Christians behave as if there is no God – because they worry and panic and get anxious. If they're right, this behaviour is completely illogical. But if there is a God, then our lives are not meaningless, and neither are our actions on this earth, because our God is a God of justice and compassion and he wants to use us to reflect these qualities to those around us.

The world in which we live, the politics that we are governed by and the events that shape our lives are temporary, but they also matter. We should not be overwhelmed, but we should live as though we can make a difference during our brief time on earth.

Case study: Fiona Bruce MP

Eighty-three per cent of the world's population live in countries where there are people who are not free to practise their faith. The charity Open Doors has calculated that roughly one in eight Christians are persecuted every day. Three hundred and sixty million Christians live in places with high levels of persecution.

Fiona Bruce's work in Parliament has been dedicated to the work of protecting religious freedom around the world. Alongside many of the other Christians in Parliament already mentioned, she is a founding member of the influential APPG for Religious Freedom and Belief, and over a year ago was made the Prime Minister's Special Envoy for Freedom of Religion and Belief.

Fiona became a Christian when, living a comfortable life with a successful legal career, she felt unfulfilled and 'utterly miserable'. Since 2010, when she went to Parliament 'with great trepidation', she has become one of the most prominent advocates of people persecuted for their religion. She works with an 'Alliance of Envoys ... from thirty-six countries across the world, and we work together to highlight instances of persecution and hopefully to be a voice for the voiceless'.

That phrase again: 'a voice for the voiceless'. It is no coincidence it has popped up throughout these case studies. As Marsha de Cordova pointed out, it is from the book of Proverbs and gets to the heart of so many Christians in politics. It is the motivating heart of Christ, and therefore of us to a much weaker extent – a heart for the vulnerable, bullied and voiceless.

Among those are religious minorities the world over. Fiona has spoken up for Rohingya Muslims in Myanmar and for Uyghurs in China. Christianity is, however, 'by far' the most persecuted religion. In her work, Fiona hears countless harrowing stories of suffering endured by our brothers and sisters in Christ. Christians are suffering from Venezuela to the Congo, from China to Nigeria.

The worst she has heard of over many years are the stories emerging from the concentration camps of North Korea. In these camps, people are worked, starved, beaten, frozen and experimented on, often until death. There are tens of thousands of Christians in these camps, sentenced for life. 'I am full of admiration . . . the bravery and the grace that they show is quite remarkable,' Fiona says.

Here in the UK we may face mockery and embarrassment. But it is nothing compared to what so many of our brothers and sisters in Christ face around the world. Fiona says that 'it is one of the most serious issues of our age'. But perhaps it is also an issue of the age to come. As Jim Shannon (another MP advocating for persecuted Christians) says, politics provides a chance for many of us 'to speak for Christians we may never meet in this age'.

After all, when faced with torture, violence, humiliation and death for themselves and their families, why would Christians cling on to faith in Christ? There is no obvious immediate gain on this earth or in this life. It must mean, then, that these people truly know that Christ is suffering alongside them as they look to a better eternal future. For two thousand years, empires and governments have tried to stamp out these awkward, stubborn believers of this strange and radical faith. They haven't succeeded yet. As Jesus says in Matthew 16:18 (ESV): 'on this rock I will build my church, and the gates of hell shall not prevail against it.'

Conclusion: Don't panic but don't duck out

What then shall we do?

At Faith in Public, we are a small group of Christians who are involved in politics. As authors of this book, we fit in that sliver of the Venn diagram where holding a biblical Christian faith coexists with political activism. We are not neutral about the Bible, nor are we neutral about whether Christians should care about politics, so if you were hoping for a balanced (on the one hand this . . . but on the other hand that . . .) approach to whether Christians should take politics seriously, then we suspect that you will have been disappointed. Indeed, you probably didn't make it far enough to read this non-apology!

We are not arguing that Christians should all rush off to join a political party, buy a rosette and a clipboard, and stand for office. Rather, the point of this book has been to consider the world of politics from a Christian perspective and to argue that Christians should be determined to care about that world. We acknowledge that politics can indeed be a mucky business teeming with vanity, greed, dishonesty, selfish ambition, hatred, godlessness and division. Yet we balance that reality against these factors:

- The rest of creation is fallen too. Politics isn't the only career or voluntary activity to be stained by sin and spoiled by similar vices. If we are going to steer clear of politics, then we would also need to steer clear of every factory, school and office too.
- We are called to love our neighbour, and that includes caring for our neighbour's well-being in this life. God clearly shows us

that our neighbour is everyone else, and given that politics affects the lives of everyone, then we cannot care for our neighbour if we don't know and care about the political decisions that affect him or her.

- We have found involvement in politics to be a means to serve others, to make personal sacrifices as we seek to meet the needs of those who may have no-one else to help them.
- How shall they hear? Politics, of course, isn't the only sphere in which people may hear the gospel, but it is nevertheless a mission field. As we understand the events guiding the life of our country or community, and as we seek practical solutions, Christians have the opportunity to live lives that bring glory to God and to earn the ability to be heard. Some of us have had many more opportunities to share the gospel as a direct result of our work in politics.

It is good for Christians to be actively involved in politics. As we said earlier, if Christians don't show up, then we can be absolutely certain that someone else will! Yet, we feel that the most important thing we can say on this matter is simply that Christians should care about current affairs and politics; they ought to be informed about political matters and to pray intelligently.

A simple summary of our case is that we must not panic about politics. We should not pin our hopes on the outcome of elections or a referendum. Instead, we should be able to hold the affairs of this world lightly, knowing that all ideologies, all parties and all governments are passing and temporary and will one day be rubble. Yet, at the same time, we should care. God cares about his creation. He loves especially deeply those whom he made in his image – and therefore so should we.

Christianity should give us the most healthy approach to the world of politics: to love others and to seek passionately to serve them but also to have the amazing peace in our hearts that comes from knowing that all this striving will soon be over and that God's perfect kingdom is at hand.

In a relatively free society such as the UK, Christians who feel marginalized by secularization should perhaps ask themselves whether they could be the solution to that problem.

By getting involved in political conversations, by being informed, by speaking and tweeting with grace on issues that we care about, we will bring ourselves in from the margins. Not that we think we should grab hold of the levers of power and usher in the new dawn of a clerical state. We will not achieve a 'Christian society' via conquest or an election win. The thought of that is terrifying! But if Christians are in the room when the council makes a decision about whether to support the Citizens Advice Bureau or to provide additional funds for a food bank, then we will be able to make a difference that people can see.

We fear that many Christians steer clear of politics because they think it involves too much moral compromise or because they see the eternal as of supreme importance and the temporary as all a bit pointless.

Our conviction is that politics is of great importance. We want Christians to understand, think about, care about, pray about and involve themselves in the political world to at least some extent.

Colossians chapter 3 reminds us that we are God's chosen people, that we are holy and dearly loved, that our salvation has already been achieved. But we then go on to learn that because of those truths we should now live our lives differently. We are told in verse 12 to 'clothe yourselves with compassion, kindness, humility, gentleness and patience'. The imagery of 'clothing yourselves' is really important to understand. When you clothe yourself, you make an effort to do it. It's a deliberate act – you are putting on something that you would not be wearing if you didn't put it on.

As a response to God's amazing grace to us in forgiving our sins because Jesus died for us, we should live differently, deliberately: 'And whatever you do, whether in word or deed, do it all in the name of the Lord Jesus, giving thanks to God the Father through him' (Colossians 3:17). We live differently by deliberately intervening in others' lives to do good and to prevent harm, because God has done us good and rescued us from harm. Politics locally and nationally gives us a route to demonstrate compassion, to serve people and to be in the room when the big discussions happen. That our culture is flawed is a given we easily accept. That every culture that has ever existed is flawed is something we sometimes overlook. Since Eden, there has been no golden age, but this is our age. In the words of Mikey from the popular 1980s film *The Goonies*: 'This is our time.'

And what shall we do with our time? Let's begin by bringing before God in prayer the issues facing our neighbours and the politicians who lead us. Let's ask God for wisdom and guidance as to how we can play our part in the public life of our community and our country. Let us clothe ourselves in compassion and love for those around us, doing so from within our church families, keeping faithful to his teaching, and constantly seeking his wisdom, guidance and grace.

Politics is a mucky business because this is a mucky world and we are mucky people . . . but we have a Saviour who calls us to serve others with a sacrificial love in response to his astonishing sacrifice and love for us. So, as we ask God to continually cleanse our hearts, let's not be afraid to get our hands dirty.

Appendix A
Why 'liberalism' should not be a dirty word

Our purpose in writing this book has been to engage and encourage Christians who may vote Conservative, SNP, Labour, Green, Plaid Cymru, Lib Dem, one of the Northern Ireland parties or – if our sales go really well – Republican or Democrat! We really haven't written (at least not consciously) from a partisan perspective. However, we're an odd bunch of people who are, broadly speaking, Christian liberals, but not liberal Christians . . . So in this appendix we want to explore why we don't think that this is an inconsistent state to be in.

'Liberalism' can be a dirty word for Christians. It is seen as the world view of our secular society, but is also divisive within the church as a brand of theology from which many evangelical Christians seek to distance themselves. However, we need to distinguish liberal theology from liberal politics. We would argue that Christians who do not follow liberal theology should nonetheless seek to uphold the values of political liberalism (which in turn is not necessarily the same as joining the Liberal Democrat Party!), because its foundations are anchored in biblical principles and because our Western political system, our 'liberal democracy', is based on it. As stewards of the land we are in until Jesus returns in glory, we must seek to do good within our cultural framework. At the same time, we would maintain that Christians should not be loyal to liberalism, or any ideology, above our loyalty to Christ. We are to be countercultural and always seek to hold our nations to account with the gospel. This means we will never fully immerse ourselves in any political ideal.

Christ's kingdom holds our ultimate loyalty, but he chooses to work through the systems and leaders of this world.

Distinction 1: liberal theology

There is an important distinction between a theologically liberal Christian and a politically liberal Christian. These days, they can often become easily muddied and confused. Although there are some parallels between theological liberalism and political liberalism, namely in the desire to engage with modernity, they are fundamentally separate ideas.

Liberal Christianity refers to the theological position within the church which emphasizes the interpretation of faith and the Bible from the standpoint of current knowledge and experience rather than that of external authority and tradition.[1] It relies on human reason and wisdom to update traditional orthodoxy, to ensure its relevance to the world today.[2] It puts weight on the humanity and some selected teachings of Jesus over some of his other teachings, on trickier biblical doctrines such as the Trinity, the divinity and resurrection of Jesus, and their cosmic implications.

The philosopher Friedrich Schleiermacher (d. 1834) is often seen as the father of liberal theology, as he first sought to reconcile the contributions and knowledge of the Enlightenment with Christian theology. He questioned our access to absolute truth, the reliability of tradition as authority, and the philosophical argument that the reason for morality can be found within our personal nature.[3] We might recognize some of his ideas when we look at the philosophical assertions of postmodernism, which we will discuss further below. For Schleiermacher, the old creeds and orthodoxy of Christian

---

1   Gary Dorrien, *The Making of American Liberal Theology: Idealism, realism, and modernity, 1900-1950* (Louisville: Westminster John Knox Press, 2003), p. xii.
2   Andrew Hoffecker, 'Liberal Theology' <https://www.thegospelcoalition.org/essay/liberal-theology> (accessed 25 July 2022).
3   John S. Knox, *Friedrich Schleiermacher: A Theological Precursor of Postmodernity?* <https://churchlifejournal.nd.edu/articles/friedrich-schleiermacher-a-theological-precursor-of-postmodernity> (accessed 25 July 2022).

doctrine fundamentally distracted from what he viewed as the most important aspects of the Christian faith: those which could actually be put into practice. These included Jesus' teachings on love, joy, compassion and peace. Furthermore, Schleiermacher rejected Christianity's claim to exclusivity of truth. He argued that there can be no consensus on what counts as 'revelation' from God, because our human capacity to understand is limited, as is our use of language. Schleiermacher believed that God would not punish those who seek him, because he knows that they are unable to achieve perfection. He stated that he could not believe in Jesus' divinity or his death as atonement because Jesus himself never expressly claimed these things. Essentially, it doesn't matter how or if you get to God, as long as you are on the journey to seeking and finding God.[4]

Schleiermacher's aim was to reshape and mould Christianity to ensure that it would stay relevant amid changes in Western culture and developments in science, and abandon the supernatural and miraculous aspects of the faith. Christianity from this perspective can be argued to have been reduced to its experience, or to the essence of the feelings it can give.

Evangelical and other orthodox Christians find liberal theology to be problematic, because doctrines such as Christ's divinity and the atoning power of his death and resurrection are fundamental to the faith. Indeed, the New Testament documents do clearly show that Jesus claimed divinity and spoke of his coming death as an atoning sacrifice, and referred to his resurrection (e.g. in Mark 8:31–35; John 10:30; 11:25–26). Any attempt to dismiss these doctrines, it is argued, is seen as removing the meaning behind the teachings of Jesus.

Being political liberals and followers of Jesus, it can be tempting to subordinate our faith to the values of pluralism and tolerance, applying and reading these truth claims in the Bible the way liberal

---

4   Knox, *Friedrich Schleiermacher.*

theology does. Therefore, it is easy to see why so many evangelicals are wary of being associated with liberalism. It is also why it is so important for us to ensure that our engagement with politics is an outpouring of our theological understanding, rather than our theology being an outpouring of our political values. In this sense, a lot of Christians are in many ways 'conservatives' when it comes to theology, since much of the faith is centred on tradition, based on what is taught in Scripture and exposited by the Apostles' Creed, being passed down since the birth of the church.[5] Liberal theology assumes that Christian doctrine and tradition is at odds with classical political liberalism and attempts to reshape it in accordance with Enlightenment views, effectively cutting political liberalism adrift from the orthodox theology that inspired its development.

Distinction 2: political liberalism

'Liberalism' is such a broad term that there is much confusion and sensitivity around its political usage. Most notable is the different use of the term in the USA (where it is often used as an insult) from the UK. In general, twenty-first-century liberalism has morphed from its British roots as it has adapted to cultural shifts in society. As a result, it has become disorientated by the widespread adoption of postmodern thought, which suggests that no ideas or claims to truth have any more merit than others. So let's seek to distinguish the core tenets and foundational principles of liberalism from the many confusing associations it has today.

It is popular to suggest that liberalism grew out of the Enlightenment – the secular humanist battle against religious attempts to suppress rationality, science and freedom. However, the founding thinker who helped develop the philosophy of liberalism in the UK and to a greater extent in the USA, John Locke (d. 1704), was acutely

---

5 Paul O'Callaghan, 'Is the Christian believer conservative or liberal?' in *Church, Communication and Culture*, Volume 4: Issue 2 (London: Taylor & Francis Group, 2019), pp. 137–151).

aware that he was fundamentally inspired by Christian theology.[6] In fact, Locke spent much time engaging and contending with what he saw as false theological justifications for the supernatural divine right of a monarch to govern a society. For example, in his *Two Treaties of Government* we see that his political philosophy was shaped by his theological understanding of the law and the doctrine of salvation.

Locke fundamentally believed that rationality and reason were gifts from God, given to enable us to rationalize between good and evil, and to discern God's law. For Locke, natural law and God's law were one and the same.[7] Unlike the secular humanist liberal perspective of the Enlightenment, Locke also upheld that some aspects of truth cannot be discovered through reason alone, but instead are made known to us through revelation.[8] In other words, we must as human beings rely on a truth which is external to us, and which we ourselves cannot rationalize or create. For Locke, philosophically, human beings are free, yet still function only within the laws of nature given by the sovereign God. It is God who gives human rights their meaning, which in the absence of a hierarchy leaves all humans in a state of total equality. This is a deeply biblical understanding: no-one is greater than another since we are all created by God in his image, but are also equally prone to sin and equally in need of salvation.

For Locke and similar liberals of his time, there are certain tenets of liberalism that cannot be violated and are natural rights which are only meaningful because they are given by God. These are the rights to life, liberty and property.[9] Within them are encompassed the more specific freedoms of thought, speech and worship.[10]

6 Roger Trigg, *Free to Believe?: Religious freedom in a liberal society* (London: Theos, 2010), p. 24.
7 'Liberalism' in *Encyclopedia Britannica* <https://www.britannica.com/topic/liberalism> (accessed 25 July 2022).
8 *Encyclopedia Britannica.*
9 *Encyclopedia Britannica.*
10 *Encyclopedia Britannica.*

Locke and many of the early liberal thinkers essentially argued that our system of justice only has meaning because human beings are the creation of God. Otherwise, it is very difficult to argue why these natural laws and rights should be upheld. If we remove God from the picture, what is it exactly that makes humans valuable or worthy of rights? The Danish philosopher Søren Kierkegaard (d. 1855) particularly emphasized the point that Christianity's contribution to philosophy was the introduction of value to the individual and the person. In this sense, a Christian is a true liberal, always seeking to defend individual liberty and dignity.[11]

The Enlightenment, despite its major positive contributions to human knowledge, had fundamentally attempted to remove the need to relate natural law, morality or humanity to God, and was largely successful in this attempt. German philosopher Friedrich Nietzsche (d. 1900) predicted huge ramifications for this argument that morality can only be discovered through human reason and the scientific revolution. The abandonment of God would leave people vulnerable to the dangers of meaninglessness: we have to try and construct meaning for society, but whose construction of meaning do we follow? In what he called the 'death of God', Nietzsche saw that order would turn to chaos, as relativism would remove any universally accepted definitions of good and evil:

> What I relate is the history of the next two centuries. I describe what is coming, what can no longer come differently: the advent of nihilism . . . For some time now our whole European culture has been moving as toward a catastrophe.[12]

Indeed, Nietzsche's predictions were right, as we saw in the twentieth century, where the supposedly most rational and progressive era of human history turned into one of the darkest periods, filled

---

11 O'Callaghan.
12 Frederich Nietzsche, *The Will to Power* (London: Penguin Classics, 2017), p. 1.

with unimaginable suffering and death inflicted upon humankind by other humans. This emphasizes that the core tenet of liberalism, as it was first conceived, was fundamentally based on the understanding that truth and morality are objective and external from us, and that not all ideas and opinions are equal. They can be rationalized only if there is a God who ultimately gives meaning to categories of right and wrong, good and evil, crime and justice. The true beauty of liberalism is not that it makes all views valid and of equal truth, but that it protects and tolerates all views so long as objective natural laws, given meaning by God, are not broken.

Today's liberalism has almost turned into the opposite, creating a culture that decides which ideas we should and should not tolerate. Postmodern philosophical trends in popular thinking have caused many to question and deconstruct much of what was fundamental to our society, even the principles of liberalism itself, redefining and reshaping it into a new idea of tolerance for progressive views and an intolerance for the things that have come before. In fact, many of our attitudes have been improved by this new trend, but it has also led to accusations of the demonization and 'cancellation' of speech that isn't deemed 'progressive' enough.

Liberals such as John Locke understood that freedom of speech is an essential part of human freedom. Of course, this should not simply give you the right to do whatever you want. There are limitations under a liberal rule of law, because my freedom ends where it compromises a greater freedom of yours. We might, for example, choose to limit freedom of speech if that speech incites violence, which would cause a greater loss of liberty. However, Christians should greatly value freedom of speech as part of the church's mandate to speak truth to power and hold the government to account. If we begin to favour speech that is only in agreement with our own perspectives and views, what is there to stop those who want to silence the Christian voice, as has been happening in countries such as Afghanistan? Tolerance doesn't mean agreeing on everything. In fact, tolerance by definition gives space for argument and disagreement, while at the same time accepting that you disagree, and agreeing to live under the same rule of law. What this doesn't mean is allowing all views to be put into practice and enshrined in law.

On one hand, it can be reasonably stated that in the UK, despite the many challenges we face as Christians in the West, we benefit greatly from the formation of a liberal society. The UK stands out when you consider the vast number of countries where freedom to believe, think and speak is not a protected right. This is not some nationalistic patriotic statement about how great the UK is. Many of us know that the church is growing faster than ever in countries where persecution is the heaviest. However, we must be aware of just how good we have it in this country. Christians are able and free to live in community and share their faith because they live in a liberal society which gives them the rights to do so. If we fail to cherish and uphold this, we risk giving up our prosperity and peace. If we are not willing to extend the right to freedom of religion or none, then we undermine the prosperity and peace that liberalism has brought us.

On the other hand, Christianity is and will always be counter-cultural. Despite having an influence on liberalism, we must hold this in tension with the fact that, ultimately, whatever system we put in place, it is not the final revelation of Jesus' kingdom. As Christians, we do not hold our ultimate allegiance to a national flag or a political movement. It is for this reason that we are called to make a stand on the things that God calls us to. If a government is abusing its God-given authority, the church has the voice to stand up against it, as a witness to the gospel and to the authority of God above human authority. We give what is the state's to the state, but we must give to God what is God's, namely ourselves. In order to fully devote ourselves to God, we must be willing to take an uncompromising stand in our obedience to his will. Our role as the church in public is to witness to what is good through how we live, and that encompasses being good citizens, but it also encompasses leading the way when we see the state moving towards an abuse of its power as given by God.

Appendix B

Who's who: the nuts and bolts of the people serving in politics

The UK Parliament

The Prime Minister (PM) and his or her team of advisers lead the direction of the government. The Leader of the Opposition leads the largest opposition party in the House of Commons, and with his or her team holds the PM to account. There are ministers in charge of every aspect of government policy, from health to defence, from foreign affairs to local government – with opposition parties appointing MPs to 'shadow' each of them and hold them to account. There are 650 MPs in the House of Commons, most of them not ministers or shadow ministers, and therefore deemed to be 'back-benchers'. Each MP represents a geographical area within the UK known as a constituency. At the other end of the Parliament building there is the House of Lords, currently with around 850 members; none of them are elected by the people, and most of them are appointed as lords for life. Both MPs and lords debate and vote on legislation and government policy.

Around Parliament there are MPs' researchers and other staff, special advisers to ministers, impartial civil servants, and staff working for MPs in their constituencies. All of these people are hugely important in shaping decisions, delivering policies, and serving and communicating with the public.

Devolved assemblies

Beyond Westminster, Scotland has its devolved Parliament with 129 elected members (MSPs), Wales has its Senedd with 60 elected members (MSs), and in Northern Ireland the Legislative Assembly has 90 elected members (MLAs). Drawn from each of these devolved assemblies, there is a government headed by the First Minister, with ministers, opposition spokespeople, and a similar range of researchers, advisers and officials to those found in Westminster.

Local government

Local government across the UK is diverse. London has its directly elected mayor and an elected London Assembly made up of 25 assembly members. Other parts of the country have a mixture of arrangements, but every place in the UK is served by at least one council and at least once elected councillor. Councillors are drawn from all walks of life; most belong to one political party or another, but many are formally independent. Although councillors are paid an allowance, for most of them it is far short of being a wage and so many will have to hold down a main job as well, although a substantial number of councillors are retired. Councillors do not tend to have advisers or researchers but are responsible for their own administration, casework and research. There are over 23,000 councillors elected to principal local authorities in the UK – in addition to thousands of members of smaller, more local and less powerful parish and community councils.

That is an army of people, all of whom are doing important work representing their communities, voting on important local issues and serving the people living in their areas.

Volunteers

Beyond those who are elected, let's remember that in order to get elected in the first place and to remain elected, MPs and all the other representatives need volunteers. As MP for my constituency in Cumbria, I estimate that I rely on around six hundred wonderful volunteers to deliver my leaflets each month. There are dozens of local coordinators, a local party Chair, Secretary and Treasurer, and many other less formal but equally important roles such as the person in charge of getting all my posters up in fields, gardens and windows during a campaign – an almost military operation! This work is unpaid, entirely voluntary and utterly essential in a campaign; at least it is if you want to win!

Abbreviations

APPG	All-Party Parliamentary Group
DWP	Department of Work and Pensions
ESV	English Standard Version
HC	House of Commons
IJM	International Justice Mission
JW	Jehovah's Witness
LGBT	lesbian, gay, bisexual, transgender
LIV	Lungisisa Indlela Village
MAGA	Make America Great Again
MLA	Member of the Legislative Assembly
MP	Member of Parliament
MS	Member of the Senedd
MSP	Member of the Scottish Parliament
NASA	National Aeronautics and Space Administration
NGO	non-governmental organization
NHS	National Health Service
NIV	New International Version
PD	Parliamentary Debate
PM	Prime Minister
SNP	Scottish Nationalist Party
UCCF	Universities and Colleges Christian Fellowship
UKIP	UK Independence Party